C

One Act Play

Poetry

Short Stories

INTRODUCTION

I met Robert Waldruff in a writing class for veterans. My first thought was that he was a tough guy. I could not guess how tough.

A young man in Chicago, he volunteered for the Marine Corps. This took him away from his bride, the daughter of a Marine general, to the jungles and conflicts of Vietnam. He survived in a way that resembles a miracle.

Robert recovered from grievous wounds, then came home. He started life with his schoolteacher wife who has loved him cross-eyed since they were newlyweds. He raised a daughter and a son of whom anyone would be proud. He built a successful accounting firm.

Later, he turned himself into a landed farmer and raised herds of bison in his fields.

In retirement, he became a memoirist, a playwright, a poet, and a photographer.

He has gone toe-to-toe with cancer.

Through it all, perhaps because of it all, Robert opened his heart wide as a sunrise to faith.

So when I say Robert is tough, I mean that he has gained a

wisdom of home, war, suffering, love, God, death and friendship that does not pander, is not hidden behind falsity or polite humility. Robert Waldruff has earned the luxury of speaking his mind. He has proven that he's worth the listen, and the read.

On these pages, you will share a lengthy exchange of letters with his daughter who, in her own adult life, figured she'd best ask Robert about Vietnam. She knows how the war changed America. She did not know how it changed her father. The letters are heartfelt and revealing. And they are strong. They were written by a Marine who cheated death.

Also in this collection is a one-act play Robert crafted for The Mighty Pen Project, a writing program for veterans, sponsored by the Virginia War Memorial. In 2021, the play was performed professionally as part of a festival of short theatrical pieces penned by veterans, called *War In Pieces*.

Robert's short stories and poems, the final part of this compendium, are an unflinching tour de force of grace and redemption. His poetry embodies the coming of God to a man who did not seek Him, yet embraced Him with all he had when the barriers broke.

I wish for you to receive from Robert Waldruff some of what I have. Sense his courage and spirit in these pages, his toughness leavened by time and empathy. You may see that, like me, you can trust him when you struggle somewhat. Robert is here in these hard-won words. I know him. He is upright. You can lean on the lessons he shares. They'll hold you up fine.

David L. Robbins, New York Times best-selling author of *Isaac's Beacon* and *War of the Rats*

FOREWORD

There are memories that can remain with a man for a half a century and more, as long as life remains. These are generally formed around family, friends, and that special group—one's comrades in war. The 244 young officers who made up the USMC Basic School Class 8-69, Hotel Company, were men who were bright, strong and ready for what our service to the nation might bring. For seven, it would lead to death in Vietnam: four United States Marines, two Republic of Korea Marines and one Republic of Vietnam Marine. In addition to these, scores were wounded, many very seriously, and several received high decorations for valor. This book details the experiences of one of those Marines, from enlistment and training, and through the test of combat.

Bob Waldruff and I went through training as Marine officers in the same classes at Quantico, Virginia and Fort Sill, Oklahoma in 1968 and 1969. In 1970 we were both assigned as artillery forward observers with the 11th Marines, in the same area of Vietnam, Quang Nam Province. The area of operations we were in was dominated by high mountains to the north and to the south, the Vu Gia river, across which was the flat plain known to Marines as The

Arizona. The area held large elements of the North Vietnamese Army and Viet Cong. It was a dangerous place, with a well-deserved reputation.

Bob and I met up on Hill 65, overlooking the Arizona and the Vu Gia. We had both been called into our battery headquarters area to prepare for some special assignments. We passed a couple of days together before going off on our separate missions. We were both filled with excitement, expectation, and a sense of adventure. When we departed, we wished each other luck, and said we would meet up again when we returned. I got back a month later. When I reported in to the battery, I learned that Bob had been seriously wounded in the Arizona and had been quickly medivaced out of country to Japan and eventually back to the United States. I had few facts about what had happened, except that it involved heavy fighting with an NVA unit, during which he was hit by shrapnel.

I did not meet with Bob again for nearly fifty years, but the memory of that last meeting remained with me. In the days before the internet, tracking people was nearly impossible, and time moves on. But preparations for a 50th anniversary reunion of our commissioning got us in contact again. Turns out that we both live in Virginia, only about fifty miles apart.

As I wrote above, there are things that a man, particularly a soldier, may carry for the rest of his life. While these experiences may be held deep inside, they are not always the things he will discuss, even with those closest to him. The families of many veterans never know the full story of what their spouses or parents have seen and done. In this book, uniquely written in an exchange of notes between a father and his daughter, Bob has described what it was like to be a Marine in Vietnam in 1970. He has answered her questions with honesty and clarity, in terms familiar to all Marine veterans of that war. I am certain that she is glad to know the answers to her questions regarding this highly important, personal, and emotional aspect of her father's life. I was privileged to read a copy of this book, and to finally know what had happened to a man I had last seen so long ago, and whose last conversation with me has remained in my memory for over five decades. You served your Corps and country well, Bob! Semper Fidelis!

COL Dennis Mroczkowski, USMC

PREFACE

I served as a Marine 1st Lieutenant in the Vietnam Conflict. With some luck, and divine grace, I survived and returned home to my wife and 6-month-old daughter, eager to put the memories behind and pursue the American Dream.

For 35 years, the memories stayed locked up deep in my soul. There were no reunions and no lasting friendships—it happened, I served, and that was that! Of course, I occasionally reminisced with pride, but very few outside my family had any interest or experience in Vietnam. Also, the conflict caused emotional division throughout the nation, so why bother dredging up past scars?

In the fall of 2007, my then thirty seven year-old daughter, Paden, born while I served in the Western Pacific, asked her mother if she thought I would mind starting, via emails, a question-and-answer reminiscence of *my* "Vietnam War." Surprised and intrigued, I immediately agreed and we started a two-and-a-half-year correspondence that explored personal and family history as well as my Vietnam tour. This journey blossomed into a wonderful exchange of love, surprise, and growth, giving us both insights into hidden corridors.

The following emails are the exchanges of our insightful indulgence and we hope they further our nation's understanding of America's Vietnam odyssey.

1

From: Paden Waldruff
Date: August 18, 2007
To: Anne F. Waldruff

Dear Mom,

Welcome home and Happy Anniversary. I hope you guys had an amazing week at the beach and thank you so much for calling me when you were there. I loved it!

I've had an idea for Dad bubbling in the back of my mind for quite some time ... and the definition finally jumped into my mind a few days ago.

It would involve Dad having an email address for personal mail and using your computer sometimes ... or maybe getting his own laptop.

Mom, could you please show Dad the following?

I want to write a book with Dad.

I have been trying to educate myself about the Vietnam War and gain a greater understanding of the past, present, and future US foreign policy. Everything I watch and read leaves me with more questions. I have the realization that I need to go further

1

back in history to understand Vietnam, an understanding that facts surrounding the war are still very sensitive and seemingly debatable, and an understanding that I, and my generation, are shamefully ignorant of the history of US foreign policy ... yet we are commenting on current events and the future of our country.

I asked Tucker at dinner tonight if Dad thought we did the right thing when we pulled out of Vietnam. He didn't know. I don't know.

I pride myself on constantly meeting new people who are very sharp, and Dad remains the smartest and most articulately opinionated man I have ever met.

I want to begin an email communication (with the thought that the correspondence could become a book if we so chose) where I can have a dialogue to teach me the truth about the Vietnam War and how it impacted my family.

2

From: Paden Waldruff
Date: September 9, 2007
To: Robert H. Waldruff

Hi Dad,

I've been thinking about you and mom and this project. One thing that is really embarrassing me is that I would describe my relationship with both of you as close. I would say I feel extremely fortunate being able to say I love you both very much, and I like you.

Suddenly, I feel like the friend who pops by all the time, eats all your food, talks only about herself ... then says "good talk, it was good to catch up with you."

I guess all parents experience that a lot ... it is a pretty thankless job.

So, we are focusing on a specific topic—your experience with the Vietnam War. Thank you for agreeing to take your time to do this with me. I can't tell you how much I appreciate it or how interested I am.

So, let's get started ... I am just cringing over my ignorance.

My impression is you were drafted? Is that correct?

If so, could you please tell me about the day you were drafted? How were you notified? How did the draft work? How old were you? Where did you live? What were you doing with your life at the time? How did you feel about the draft and the war before you became personally involved, and did those feelings change after you became personally involved?

If I've been wrong all these years in my belief that you were drafted, could you please tell what did happen?

3

From: Robert H. Waldruff
Date: September 13, 2007
To: Paden Waldruff

Paden,

Please don't think I've ignored your initial inquiry. Your questions require thought and I want to get it right. Your interest in this topic and my experience intrigues me. It is the first (and probably only) time someone with an intellectual curiosity plus a true caring interest for me has ever asked, "What did you do during the war?" There have been many who asked to be polite (not really caring about my answers), and some have asked to find out what it was like, as a freak show at the carnival. When I talk to other vets it seems they don't want to revisit, are afraid I'll find out they really weren't in the trenches, and/or have moved on. There were over five million people who served in Vietnam in some capacity (the war lasted ten years) and obviously many never saw combat and many saw brutality too gruesome to discuss. I probably fall in the middle, as I saw combat but did not see a lot of killing.

More directly, to your questions: I was raised without a whole lot of discussion or knowledge of what military life was all about. My father was one of the few of his generation who never wore a uniform in WWII and I'm not really sure why not. Maybe he felt guilty about this, and that could be why he never discussed this with me. However, I did see John Wayne movies and was raised to wave the flag and love America. Also, since I grew up knowing there was a universal draft, I just always knew part of my life would be spent in uniform and I looked forward to serving my country. All males on their eighteenth birthday had to register with the Draft Board and get their selective service card (I still have mine). When I started at the University of Virginia, I signed up for Navy ROTC and took classes my first year . . . I got a uniform and everything, thinking that when I graduated, I would serve as a naval officer. I never felt that I would wait and see if I would be drafted. I just always knew when the time came, drafted or not, I would sign up and get on with it. Being a Marine was certainly never on my agenda.

During my second year at UVA (1963-1964), I quit Naval ROTC. I think the reasons were: I hated it, didn't want to take the obligatory six-week ship cruise during the upcoming summer, and I thought it was useless as when I graduated, I would just join the Navy anyway and didn't need to waste my time during college. My exit interview was with a Marine Major (you know that the Marines, much to their displeasure, are a part of the Navy). I later found out he was a friend of your grandfather, BaBa. He said I could be making a big mistake because when I graduated there could be a war going on, and I could be shut out of the Navy (a war going on—was this guy nuts or what?).

The Gulf of Tonkin incident occurred in August 1964, and President Johnson (who was elected president in November 1963, stating he would not "send American boys 7,000 miles away to fight an Asian war") now said we were sending in a contingent of Marines to guard the airbase at Da Nang. Thus the ten year "conflict" began. I was just finishing my third year at UVA.

As the war grew in casualties and number of troops on the ground, it started to dominate news headlines and national discourse. During my last year at UVA, I can't say it dominated conversation, but being draft-eligible, we were all aware of what was going on. At this time there were many draft-deferments available, e.g., married with children, graduate student, teacher, and of course the rich-boy's out, that is, the local National Guard unit (as President George W. Bush did). So, it was pretty rare to know someone who was going to, or had gone, to Vietnam.

As Mom and I were seeing quite a bit of each other, and a lot of her friends were dating Marines from the Officer's Basic School at Quantico, I got to know some guys who were heading over. I still just felt that when the time came, I would join the Navy and serve as an officer (whether drafted or not). I applied to the University of Pennsylvania's Wharton School and University of Chicago MBA programs, and was wait-listed at Chicago. In June 1966, just prior to my UVA graduation, Chicago notified me I was accepted, thus delaying any move to join the military. In September 1966, I started the master's program at Chicago, and Mom started her final year at Mary Washington College. The war was increasing in intensity, and a majority of the country supported it. We talked about it from time to time at Chicago, but we were the "best and the brightest" and surely would find some way to avoid going to Vietnam.

I can't say I wanted to go to Vietnam, but I felt increasingly dedicated to serving and was not looking for a loophole out of serving. I remember, to this day, drinking beer at the Woodlawn Tap with some classmates, and we mused—was there anything worth dying for? The group said no, and I said fighting for America's freedom was. (Was I naive or crazy?) 1967 moved on and I was young and in love. We married in August and moved into our three-bedroom apartment in the western suburbs of Chicago. Mom was teaching Spanish at a junior high, and I was commuting to graduate school. The mood of the country was becoming more anti-war, and demonstrations were becoming common events. In February 1968, the Tet offensive occurred in Vietnam. As history later revealed, the US killed a huge amount of Viet Cong and NVA (North Vietnamese Army) soldiers, severely hurting their war effort. The US pundits dwelled on the US casualties, and Walter Cronkite concluded we could not win in Vietnam. (Sound familiar?) A whole new wave of anti-war protests was staged. They were much more violent than before. In April 1968, Martin Luther King was assassinated, and several cities, including Chicago, had riots and massive fires. The National Guard was called out in Chicago, and I went to classes downtown with armed army troops and barricades on street corners (like in the movies). Just when all this disruption was waning, Bobby Kennedy was assassinated in June. The nation went through another convulsion, and the headlines continued to criticize the Vietnam "War."

I tell you all this to set the scene for when I was drafted in May 1968 (yes, your memory is correct, I was drafted). The notice came in the mail to our apartment, and said I had 60 days (I think it was 60) to report for my physical. The May date was no coincidence as it seems the US government sent out draft notices to all eligible candidates due to the Tet Offensive and the perceived need for many more US troops. I was two months shy of my 24th birthday. As I stated, I was not particularly alarmed or surprised, as I planned to serve regardless. All of my Chicago classmates who were drafted went to a National Guard unit in the Southside of Chicago, and signed-up for the seven-year weekend warrior tour, knowing they would most likely never go to Vietnam. I took the Navy entrance exam, and did not pass. The Navy had so many applicants that no one was passing the exam at this time—thus the Marine Major's warning became reality. I next went to the Air Force, but they required a five-year commitment, and said I wouldn't qualify to fly because I needed glasses.

Not wanting to serve more than the three-year minimum I

went to the Army (Notice the Marines were not my first choice! I believed in the war, but I was not suicidal.) Their program was nine months as a private, training at five different bases, without wives. Left with no other choice, I went to see the Marine recruiter— "Have I got a deal for you!" Marine OCS (Officer Candidates School) was only ten weeks, after which you were commissioned a 2nd Lieutenant. Your wife could join you for the twenty-week Basic School at Quantico, and you were paid as an officer. I signed up that day! A huge relief came over me, as I had made my decision to support America and the war. I made Mom proud, BaBa was taking a renewed interest in me, and I was becoming excited about being a Marine. Grandma and Grandpa never really told me what they felt, but I don't think they shared my enthusiasm.

I took the physical and was told I would get orders to Quantico and OCS in November 1968. After I graduated from Chicago in August, Mom and I went to California, and we lived with Grandma and Grandpa until I reported to duty in November.

4

From: Paden Waldruff
Date: September 13, 2007
To: Robert H. Waldruff

Dear Dad:

I definitely didn't think that you were ignoring my initial inquiry. I assumed, as is the case, that you were thinking carefully about your response. I have learned over the years that I am rare and fortunate to have an extremely strong, intelligent, responsible father who actually took the time to deal with my painful, formative years, for better or for worse.

I've read what you've written over and over again. I have a thought and question about every line. My line of thinking is influenced tonight by childhood memories I think I have, but I'm not sure if I trust them.

I feel completely shocked by how young you were. I don't want to ask questions about what you've written right now. I want you to please continue. You left off in November of 1968, when you and Mom were in California with Grandma and Grandpa, waiting to report for duty.

Where/what was home with your parents at that time? How did Mom fit in? Were Larry and Sandy around, too? What were Grans and The General saying? I can't imagine what that waiting period must have been like. I don't even know where you reported for duty. I am trying to remember now what Mom told me about where Marine officers go. I am not going to embarrass myself by guessing.

Please don't feel rushed in responding, or that you need to move quickly through details.

5

From: Robert H. Waldruff

Date: September 19, 2007

To: Paden Waldruff

Paden,

First let me clear up some facts from the last response. Johnson became President in November 1963, after the JFK assassination. The Gulf of Tonkin incident, which officially began the Vietnam Conflict (it was never called a war by the politicians) occurred in August 1964 and Johnson was elected in November 1964. He took office in January 1965, and sent in the Marines in March 1965.

Mom and I left Chicago in August with all our life's possessions stuffed in our 1964 red Ford Falcon convertible. We took our time going West and went through Nebraska, Wyoming, Nevada, San Francisco, and down the Pacific Coast Highway (Route 101) to Los Angeles. The car was so packed we literally could not see out the back windows.

As I later came to realize, Mom was miserable most of the time in California. We lived in the penthouse at the Sojourn Motel that Grandma and Grandpa owned. It was about a mile from LAX.

There was nothing close by of interest to Mom, i.e., no shopping, parks, museums, restaurants, etc., but it *was* close to some pretty rough neighborhoods, so she couldn't even go for walks.

I worked full time with my father at the Sojourn and his other motel, The Arroyo Inn, in Pasadena. I was enjoying myself, was busy helping my parents, and pretty much enjoying the variety offered by working at a motel. Grandma and Grandpa lived in Torrance, as did Sandy and John. Larry was a senior in high school. Mom and I spent most weekends with Grandma and Grandpa and Sandy and John. You get the picture—Mom had nothing to do but watch TV, eat, and hang out with the Waldruffs.

Needless to say, she gained about thirty pounds and was pretty miserable. To her credit she did not complain much. I guess we both knew this was a short-term arrangement. In retrospect, I probably should have tried to stay in Chicago, but I thought it would be great to be in Southern California and be with my family for a few months before my life was to change drastically—so much for 20/20 hindsight. Believe it or not, even though Vietnam dominated the headlines we did not talk much about it, or about my fast-approaching date with the USMC. In fairness, my parents were so unaware of military life, and no-doubt worried about me, that they didn't know what to say or ask. Mom and I didn't talk much about it either—young and fearless!

The early days with Grans and BaBa did not involve a lot of communication. We lived in Chicago and they lived in Falls Church,

Virginia, and we talked periodically by phone. They didn't really know me, and vice versa. I knew they weren't thrilled with me as a son-in-law. Grans and her friend Nina Platt would tell Mom during our courtship that they wished she would date one of those "cute" Marine Captains stationed at Headquarters Marine Corps. BaBa, although always polite and respectful, was not particularly warm and frequently would ask Mom what I was going to do for our country. He thought that I was probably going to grad school, that I would dodge the draft like most civilian pukes of my generation. He never told me, but I'm pretty sure he was pleasantly shocked when we called him from Chicago after I signed up with the USMC.

I don't know for sure, but based on comments during our lives, I think Grans felt I did it to please BaBa. In July 1968, BaBa (who was then a Colonel) was assigned to the Marine Corp Barracks at 8th & I Streets in Washington DC. This is a coveted duty, in charge of the Commandant's Home, and an almost sure stepping stone to Brigadier General.

My orders were to report to Marine OCS on, as I remember, November 9, 1968. Mom and I packed up our Falcon and left California around October 28. We took the southern route, saw the Grand Canyon, etc ..., and headed for DC. I think during this trip we started to realize a separation was looming, and that we faced a lot of unknowns, but—onward to our destiny!

6

From: Paden Waldruff

Date: September 19, 2007

To: Robert H. Waldruff

Dear Dad:

My ignorance astounds and humiliates me. Yet even when one is truly interested in learning the facts of the Vietnam "conflict," details are slippery. From the documentaries I've been watching, I am under the impression that there were two Gulf of Tonkin incidents. I am also under the impression that the second was the inflammatory event, and that hindsight shows it was misrepresented or didn't occur. Is that true?

And in this part of the personal story, you guys were rad newlyweds. "Rad" is the word all of my super-hip artists use. "Rad," short for radical, but meaning cool ... not radical in a '60s way. I can easily picture you bombing down the open highway in the red Ford Falcon convertible, but I am struggling with my image of Mom driving cross country. I guess that is why the car was so jammed with stuff; that is my sole Mom identifier.

She obviously really loved you, Dad. And, I hope neither of

you would feel offended by the following, but you and Mom were ridiculously young. One of the things that irritates me these days is prolonged adolescence—adult teenagers. Our old friend Coach and I talked a lot about this sad statement on society. Meaning that by today's standards you and Mom were very young. But dear God, should children be coddled indefinitely? Is 35 the new 25 for being personally responsible? Sad. In so many ways, I cannot believe all of the challenges you have faced together and that you made it. Wow.

And it makes complete sense to me that you would want to spend your time with your family before you left for Vietnam. I've heard bits and pieces of the stories from that period. I still laugh to myself sometimes when I picture Larry delivering the breakfast to an empty room. What was it ... Blueberry Baby or something? When you and John were laughing around the corner. Classic Waldruff humor. And Mom worked the switchboard? But I never connected them to your imminent departure.

I've gone on long enough. Please continue when you have time, and please don't rush. Every word you are writing is incredibly interesting to me.

So, thank you for your time,

P

7

From: Robert H. Waldruff
Date: September 26, 2007
To: Paden Waldruff

To provide more background—during the time I was drafted in May 1968, the same month that campuses throughout America held war moratorium demonstrations, including sit-ins, storming the President's office, etc., The University of Chicago canceled all classes one day and held a big protest march concluding with a rally and speech by Muhammad Ali (who ended up serving jail time for refusing to enlist upon being drafted). I used it as a day to catch up on studies, and didn't get too excited about it one way or another.

Obviously, to serve or not serve was a huge decision and statement for each draftee. Many went to Canada, which provided sanctuary. I thought these people were cowards, as many others bit the bullet and did jail time for their decision. Much later, in 1977, President Jimmy Carter's first official proclamation upon being inaugurated was to grant blanket amnesty to all draft dodgers, thus tainting all who served and all who paid a price by going to jail. These facts are also why I found Bill Clinton's lies to his draft board reprehensible. It's not like we all didn't have to face the music, which most Americans did with integrity and honor. Either way, there was a price to pay for either decision. Clinton, as with everything in his life, wanted it both ways without cost.

In August 1968, right before Mom and I left for California, the Democratic National Convention was held in Chicago. This was very contentious from the get-go. LBJ said he would not seek another term, and his heir apparent was Hubert H. Humphrey, the Vice President. Humphrey came with all of Johnson's baggage, and was considered pro-war by the left-wing fanatics. The challenger for the Democratic nomination was Eugene McCarthy, who had defeated LBJ in the New Hampshire primary.

The Convention was in downtown Chicago, and turned into a circus with all the left-wing loonies holding protest rallies at Grant Park just off the loop. Jerry Rubin and Tom Hayden (who later married Jane Fonda and became a California lawmaker) and other hippies and yippies were there, as were Bobby Seale and Angela Davis with their Black Panther thugs, and thousands of other protesters.

All this mayhem ended when Mayor Daley sent Chicago's Finest, armed with billy clubs, into the shantytown set up by protestors in a large park. They beat hundreds of protestors to a bloody pulp. The week ended with the famous Chicago Seven trial, during which the judge gagged and tied Seale to his chair. This whole episode became known as "the Days of Rage." Vietnam gripped the nation, and remains the defining moment of my generation.

Mom and I often reflect how our relationship strengthened from living alone our first year away from family, making all our own decisions. We grew up on our own, together, and in love. I think you get a sense why I feel so strongly that veterans' wives deserve recognition. Vietnam was shared jointly by a married couple with different emotions, fears, and personal thoughts.

Before graduation, I accepted a job with GT&E International (General Telephone & Electronics Corporation, now GTE), to be trained and assigned as a controller of one of their overseas manufacturing plants. My starting date would be right after discharge from the USMC. Price Waterhouse made a great offer, but I felt it was time to move on even though I had interned for six months.

8

From: Paden Waldruff

Date: September 26, 2007

To: Robert H. Waldruff

Again … flabbergasted.

I simply can't imagine a university canceling classes for a protest. Cannot imagine a university ceding control. I cannot.

How very strange that your generation, the children of WWII, directly challenged institutions. And my generation maintains a strange faith in them, often masked as a childish entitlement?

What did you think of BaBa endorsing Joey in his plans to head for Canada if the draft was reinstated? I was horrified.

And what do you and the Baby Boomers think of all the disintegration that has happened in one generation? All around me I see people my age and younger looking for a quick fix, or a trick guerilla response, or any excuse to avoid being an adult by the traditional definition. How did this happen? Why and when did America lose its work ethic and values?

I only want to make this very brief aside, but the media isn't helping. It really doesn't help when the people who are up and getting ready to walk out the door at 7 a.m. for work, the people on a W-2 and funding Social Security and the looming universal health care plan, are treated to the *Today Show*, bringing us as their lead story of the day, that Britney Spears got drunk at a club last night in LA. I'm sorry, is that news? Are we not at war? You have to dig pretty deep to find real news, and frankly, my generation is too damn lazy to do that work.

How did we disintegrate so quickly?

And, back to the fascinating personal story. What if things had turned out differently, if you and Mom had decided to move overseas to work for GT&E. What?

9

From: Robert H. Waldruff
Date: October 3, 2007
To: Paden Waldruff

Paden,

As we move ahead with this saga, you need to keep in perspective that although I'll try to be as honest as possible about my thoughts at the time, they will obviously be tainted by what's happened over the past forty years, by what I know now, and by what I did not know then. After thinking about it, we left California after the presidential election of 1968. I remember watching the late-night results with my father, happy that Nixon would defeat Humphrey and that the Republicans would regain control of the White House. Thus, we would have left California around the 8th of November. I probably started OCS around the 18th. Also—very important fact—we traded the red Falcon convertible for a champagne-gold Ford Fairlane station wagon. I was sinking further into marriage-dom.

The Vietnam Conflict was controversial from the beginning. In the early '60s the Cold War with Russia was raging. Communism was our enemy, and Russia dropping the bomb was our fear. In 1954, the French lost the battle of Dien Bien Phu to the North Vietnamese giving the NVA control in Southeast Asia. We became fearful that the NVA, with backing from Russia, would move against the nations of Southeast Asia. That would turn them into a Communist stronghold, backed by Russia against the US, thus forcing us politically and economically out of that part of the Pacific. This would occur with the NVA taking over South Vietnam first, and then like "dominoes" the rest of the countries would fall.

At this time we had a young, inexperienced President (JFK) who was being tested by Russia to see how tough he was, e.g., the Missile Crisis in Cuba in 1962. Our ambassador in South Vietnam told Kennedy that the current president of South Vietnam (Diem) was a Communist sympathizer. He had to be eliminated, as the NVA were infiltrating the South more and more. We needed a strong pro-democracy leader. Thus, JFK authorized the assassination of Diem, and a coup to put our boy Thieu in control. This has been debated forever since, whether we would have been better off to have Diem in power.

Regardless, during 1963 we started sending military advisors to help the Army of South Vietnam (ARVN) organize and fight the NVA infiltrators. This was a slow process, and was producing few positive results. The NVA was a well-trained and large army, and the ARVN was the opposite. So, the US was trying to provide more and more support without looking like we were interfering in South Vietnamese domestic affairs. They wouldn't invite us in because of political reasons. While these issues were being analyzed, supposedly the NVA's Navy attacked two of our ships in the Gulf of Tonkin, declaring we had violated their territorial waterway. I think one of the ships was the Turner Joy (pretty good, if I correctly remembered this). Johnson immediately called this an act of aggression against the US. He had his excuse to send in US troops, which he did.

Thus, the ageless controversy has been whether the US trumped up this event to justify sending in troops. Or, did the NVA actually do this, trying to intimidate us to see if we would respond with force, or retreat. I'm not sure this has ever been factually resolved. All I knew was that the Communists were trying to take over Southeast Asia, and were feasting on a peaceful democratic neighbor that was unable to defend itself. The NVA was attacking our military; we had to help.

Your comments about how young we were, particularly compared to your generation, are interesting. I truly think it's a generation thing. My parents' generation did things in their teens we wouldn't have done. Our generation went to college, got married, settled down, got a job, raised a family, and got on with things. The Vietnam Conflict caused some adjustments in this life-plan. As far as the modern day press, you need to remember a lot of them were draft resisters during Vietnam. They have spent their lives trying to rationalize to themselves, and to America, that their decision was not only not cowardly, but was actually patriotic. I think there is a huge amount of guilt; thus the ongoing attempt to denigrate the military.

10

From: Paden Waldruff
Date: October 10, 2007
To: Robert H. Waldruff

Dear Dad:

I've read this over and over again. I tried taking notes while I was reading, to try to collect my thoughts. Finally I've settled on the rude email technique of basically interrupting you with more questions.

RW: As we move ahead with this saga, you need to keep in perspective that although I'll try to be as honest as possible about my thoughts at the time, they will obviously be tainted by what's happened over the past forty years, by what I know now, and by what I did not know then. After thinking about it, we left California after the presidential election of 1968. I remember watching the late-night results with my father, happy that Nixon would defeat Humphrey and that the Republicans would regain control of the White House. Thus, we would have left California around the 8th of November. I probably started OCS around the 18th.

PW: So you were raised Republican? How did Grandpa become a Republican? How did Aunt Lou become such a Democrat? And I've always had the feeling that The General was a Democrat at heart? Did I completely make that up?

And where was OCS?

RW: Also—very important fact—we traded the red Falcon convertible for a champagne-gold Ford Fairlane station wagon. I was sinking further into marriage-dom.

PW: Cringe.

RW: The Vietnam Conflict was controversial from the beginning. In the early '60s the Cold War with Russia was raging. Communism was our enemy, and Russia dropping the bomb was our fear.

PW: You are my Dad, and we Waldruffs love a good poke in the ribs for stupid comments, even if I cover my ignorance when I am with my fancy people. I am thrilled to have a chance to learn.

So the '60's is where I start getting lost. I was taught WWII and the fortress mentality that followed in the fifties. I assume "communism" translates to Russia. I remember Dr. Satterwhite teaching me at Freeman to "never underestimate the power of the Russians." But I don't totally understand the escalation to garden-variety citizens in the US fearing bombs from Russia. Even if I just made an overstatement, I am still unclear. Russian Communism was aggressive enough and determined enough to try to take over the world? Sounds like hyperbole, but you get my point.

RW: In 1954, the French lost the battle of Dien Bien Phu to the

North Vietnamese giving the NVA control in Southeast Asia. We became fearful that the NVA, with backing from Russia, would move against the nations of Southeast Asia. That would turn them into a Communist stronghold, backed by Russia against the US, thus forcing us politically and economically out of that part of the Pacific. This would occur with the NVA taking over South Vietnam first, and then like "dominoes" the rest of the countries would fall.

At this time we had a young, inexperienced President (JFK) who was being tested by Russia to see how tough he was, e.g., the Missile Crisis in Cuba in 1962. Our ambassador in South Vietnam told Kennedy that the current president of South Vietnam (Diem) was a Communist sympathizer. He had to be eliminated, as the NVA were infiltrating the South more and more. We needed a strong pro-democracy leader. Thus, JFK authorized the assassination of Diem, and a coup to put our boy Thieu in control. This has been debated forever since, whether we would have been better off to have Diem in power.

PW: Regardless of whether he was right or wrong, were we seen as weak in how it was handled? I am under the impression that the answer is yes.

RW: Regardless, during 1963 we started sending military advisors to help the Army of South Vietnam (ARVN) organize and fight the NVA infiltrators. This was a slow process, and was producing few positive results. The NVA was a well-trained and large army,

PW: Trained by Russia? Self-trained?

RW: and the ARVN was the opposite. So, the US was trying to provide more and more support without looking like we were interfering in South Vietnamese domestic affairs. They wouldn't invite us in because of political reasons. While these issues were being analyzed, supposedly the NVA's Navy attacked two of our ships in the Gulf of Tonkin, declaring we had violated their territorial waterway. I think one of the ships was the Turner Joy (pretty good, if I correctly remembered this). Johnson immediately called this an act of aggression against the US. He had his excuse to send in US troops, which he did.

Thus, the ageless controversy has been whether the US trumped up this event to justify sending in troops. Or, did the NVA actually do this, trying to intimidate us to see if we would respond with force, or retreat. I'm not sure this has ever been factually resolved. All I knew was that the Communists were trying to take over Southeast Asia, and were feasting on a peaceful democratic neighbor that was unable to defend itself. The NVA was attacking our military; we had to help.

PW: Yes, it is amazing what I read about this, and how whatever I read about this is criticized/analyzed.

RW: Your comments about how young we were, particularly compared to your generation, are interesting. I truly think it's a generation thing. My parents' generation did things in their teens we wouldn't have done. Our generation went to college, got married, settled down, got a job, raised a family, and got on with things. The Vietnam Conflict caused some adjustments in this life-plan. As far as the modern day press, you need to remember a lot of them were draft resisters during Vietnam. They have spent their lives trying to rationalize to themselves, and to America, that their decision was not only not cowardly, but was actually patriotic. I think there is a huge amount of guilt; thus the ongoing attempt to denigrate the military.

PW: I worry, don't you? Your parents took on responsibility in their teens (for better or worse). Your generation took on responsibility in its twenties (for better or worse). My generation delays, delays, delays. Forty year-old, ignorant, lazy, mouthing-off, adult-teenagers are the norm. Dear God.

I can't even hazard an adjective to describe my generation for the following comment. But your generation was mobilized for the threat of communism, and to protect our homeland without a major catastrophe occurring on our soil. My generation was raised in your generation's homes, yet we seem (again searching for the adjective... none positive) naive to the fact that a major invasion did happen on our soil.

What in the world happened? Draft dodgers taking over the media? I am not joking; something trashed journalism.

Looking forward to your next thoughts—historical and personal.

XO,

P

11

From: Robert H. Waldruff
Date: October 17, 2007
To: Paden Waldruff

Paden,

At this rate we'll never get to Vietnam! Yes, I was raised in a very Republican and politically conservative family. I guess my father was more into politics than my mother. Back then most of Illinois, outside of Chicago (I was raised in Homewood, just south of the city) was Republican. It's changed a lot now. Having been raised in Chrisman, a small farming town, also influenced my father's beliefs. Primarily, like me, he resented government interference into our lives, believed in freedom of choice for all Americans, and thought FDR was the worst president in history because he started so many government programs that were all part of the New Deal, primarily Social Security and farm subsidies.

My sophomore year in high school, our history teacher (who was very liberal) assigned us a paper on which president was the best, and which was the worst. I wrote that FDR was the worst, and why I thought so. I got a D, and Grandpa had a parent-teacher conference to tell the guy he was all wet. That probably didn't help my reputation in the teacher's lounge. Point being, he was passionate about it. When Ike was elected President in 1952 as a Republican, the first republican in 36 years, Grandpa took our family to D.C. for the inauguration.

Aunt Lou became a Democrat when she went to work at one of FDR's big programs, the Tennessee Valley Authority. Its mission was to develop the Tennessee River with dams, etc., to help the economy of rural Tennessee. This is where she met Aunt Mary and most of her other DC cronies, as they all moved to DC from Knoxville to TVA headquarters. Thus, she was forever grateful to FDR and the government for giving her a career and opportunity that she didn't think a woman of that time could get anywhere else. Plus, Aunt Lou always had a soft spot for the "little guy." Back then, the Democratic party advertised itself as the party of the little guy, and the Republicans represented the "fat cats." A bunch of hooey, but she and a lot of other people believed it.

Don't know about The General. You may be right, but I never thought the Fegans were into politics. A military officer is supposed to be apolitical; that's also changed today. The whole Nixon deal was a great smear job by the liberals. To this day, it muddied the water with untruths and influenced a lot of voters to go Democrat. Thus we got the worst president in history, Jimmy Carter. Anyway, Nixon was President from 1968 to 1974.

OCS was and is at Quantico, Virginia. It's one of many things making the USMC unique. All Marine officers go to OCS and to six months of Basic School at Quantico. This ensures quality and continuity of training for all officers, and gives each officer common ground, a shared experience with every other officer regardless of age.

After WWII, the victors carved up the spoils at the Yalta Conference, with FDR, Stalin, and Churchill thus setting the stage for the forty-year Cold War. At this conference, Korea was split into two countries. Likewise Vietnam was divided by a geographically established Demilitarized Zone (DMZ). During these forty years it was a matter of wills between democratic and communist societies for world supremacy—the age of propaganda, threats (both verbal and military), and misinformation. There was indeed a true fear of WWIII between the Communists led by the USSR and the democracies led by the US.

All this was the basis for the fear of a first-strike nuclear bomb. Thus, the various ensuing confrontations were always played out in the context of this bigger possibility—the Cuban Missile Crisis, the Suez War, the Six-Day War in the Middle East, the Korean War, the Vietnam Conflict, etc. The other big Communist country was China, under Chairman Mao, and even more remote and fanatical than Russia. China, although Communist, was no friend of Russia. But there was a fear they would go to war and force us in. When Russia launched Sputnik in 1956, fear and panic swept America. We felt we'd fallen behind, and that Russia might attack us from space. Thus the rush to set up NASA and all the astronaut programs, to regain our lead in space, and protect us from attack. I'm not saying America didn't sleep at night. But just as today we live with constant fear of another terrorist attack, back then we lived with the fear of a nuclear war with Russia. Russia was indeed aggressive and expansionist. Witness the Hungarian Revolt, and Russia's perpetual intervention into "neutral" nations. They try to help other Communists destabilize their governments, and then stage a coup to set up a Communist regime. Think of Cambodia, Thailand, Indonesia, Panama, Nicaragua, etc.

I don't think the US was seen as weak during the early phase of Vietnam by either Americans or Russians. The NVA was trained and funded by Russia, as a total Communist partner against the US and democratic governments. Thus, the Domino Theory. With Russian backing, Ho Chi Minh and the NVA could conquer and spread Communism to all of Indo-China. Concerning our intervention into Vietnam, there was also a treaty violation by the NVA (SEATO). They infiltrated the DMZ, and the US was a signatory of the Yalta agreement forbidding such action. Were we to abandon our allies, having promised support by written commitment?

Your observation about my generation being willing to go 7,000 miles away to fight to protect America's freedom, and your generation not willing to fight even after the homeland has been attacked, is interesting. You must temper this with the fact that not all of my generation was willing to go. A lot of your generation has served or is serving in the military. But I do fear we're heading for a situation where, for whatever reason, we will lose our will to fight for anything. "Here, you can have it. Just leave me alone so I don't have to think about it."

The glamour jobs sought by University of Chicago MBAs in 1968 were investment banking and/or something overseas. Mom and I were quite satisfied with spending time in Madrid, etc. getting my career started. Remember, we had no children and were carefree!

You can't call most of what on TV pretends to be news reporting, "journalism." It's political commentary with no attempt to be objective or truthful.

12

From: Paden Waldruff
Date: October 17, 2007
To: Robert H. Waldruff

Dear Dad:

Oh God, Dad, you are so right.

I can't believe you brought up FDR. I just listened to an hour-long show on NPR (Yes, I spend most of my time educating myself on how the other side thinks) during which an expert expressed opinions (that is the key word) very different from yours and your father's. I couldn't believe what he was saying. You have to have strong convictions and a strong desire for self-education to see your way past "experts." Here is where I start worrying about my passive generation again.

Tempted as I am to ask more questions about everything you've said, globally and about our family, because your responses are so amazing, I agree.

Please continue. You said you left California for OCS in November, right?

13

From: Paden Waldruff

Date: October 17, 2007

To: Robert H. Waldruff

Dear Dad:

Oh, and, you know better than anyone that I am a born pest. I have tried mightily to contain it as I've matured. Any progress I've made is a sincere homage to you for putting up with me at my worst. I actually just started laughing when I thought to myself that the time frame I am referencing, the time frame when I was a child and accepted no personal responsibility for my actions, was two decades long. Emphasis on the word "long." All when you had a lot of other responsibilities, goals, etc. to tend to. Where I laughed, I am sure you grimaced. How did you refrain from strangling me?

14

From: Robert H. Waldruff
Date: October 30, 2007
To: Paden Waldruff

Paden,

Ask all the questions you want, no matter how trivial you may think they are. This may be your only chance, and I'm fascinated by them.

Yes, we left on the journey sometime in the middle of November, with Mom and me heading east in our brand-spanking-new Ford Fairlane station wagon. During this trip we made a side trip to the Grand Canyon. Of course every time I see the Canyon, I'm in awe. This time was particularly beautiful as we headed back to the main road through a pine forest near Flagstaff as it was snowing. This just a few days after leaving the heat and smog of LA.

BaBa was selected for Brigadier General in September. He and Grans left Washington for his new duty as Assistant Commander of the 2nd Marine Division, stationed at Camp Lejeune, NC Mom and I saw Aunt Lou and my college friend, Renny Barnes. We had a small party at his apartment in Arlington, and Mom and I spent the night there. The next day Mom dropped me off at OCS-Quantico. She headed to Camp Lejeune to stay with the parents until I, hopefully, completed OCS. Then she could join me while I attended The Basic School at Quantico. She dropped me off around 4 p.m. on a cloudy, cold, and rainy November day. I got out of the car, kissed her goodbye, and off she went.

I was immediately shouted at by a Sergeant (might as well have been a General for all I knew) to get in line and get to the barber shop. A different, new, and strange world surrounded me. Uniformed Marines shouting and recruits scrambling around, trying, with apprehensive faces, to obey the various commands. Hair was cut and we "marched" to our new home for the next ten weeks, a barracks on the Potomac River. Of course none of us knew how to march, and we were still in civilian clothes. There were many different groups marching to their new homes in different barracks. In retrospect, I'm quite certain this must have been one of the most humorous days for the instructors, watching a bunch of civilian dorks trying to figure out what was going on.

We got into the barracks and into our squad-bay. There were probably 30 metal bunk beds down each side of the large room, with a wide aisle in the middle. Several recruits were standing at attention next to their beds. Each pair of bunkmates shared a metal locker placed at the end of the bed. We new arrivals were assigned our bunk, and told to empty our pockets onto our beds. Fortunately, I didn't have anything too unusual to "display", as the instructors were quick to ridicule anything too civilian. We then surrendered any sport coats and/or jackets and sweaters. All this was removed to storage, and there we stood at attention waiting for the next group to arrive and submit to their indoctrination.

I noticed several recruits were in white T-shirts and green Marine utility trousers. They were also at attention. Though they seemed savvier than us, they were definitely not instructors. What I found out later, much to my horror that such a thing could happen, is that these recruits were "recycles." That meant that for whatever reason (couldn't handle the physical requirements, couldn't transform to military from civilian, etc.), they were required to start OCS over and endure another ten weeks. Also to my sheer panic, I found out that recruits deemed unable to shape up even after being recycled were bused off to Parris Island. They had to serve out their enlistment as an enlisted Marine. Yikes, what have I gotten myself into? I always assumed that if for some reason I didn't hack it, I would be discharged. No one ever said I would be made a private, given a rifle, and sent off to Vietnam.

As I'm sure you know, the purpose of OCS is twofold: one, to break you down from your civilian comfort zone and, through brainwashing techniques, to rebuild you as a Marine both physically and mentally, and two, to weed out those who could not hack it. I was never intimidated by this process, as I could usually see the purpose of the oral harassment, etc. I found most of the instructors fair and professional. The key to survival was not to f-up, and not to stand out; keep clean and get through. I saw several recruits break down and cry. It was obviously better to weed these types out at OCS rather than on some battlefield.

A lot of what happened was humorous, but I truly hated every aspect of it. For openers, sharing a barracks, bathroom, and shower with fifty-plus strangers was invasive. And until you went to sleep at night, somebody was always in your face shouting instructions. There was absolutely no privacy, ever. We were not given any weekend leave until December, although we got Thanksgiving off. We could go to a bar in Quantico Town, but could not leave the base. We were given our Marine utilities (green shirt & green trousers). They taught us, for hours at a time, to march in formation. And we were given a lot of physical training. I got a couple of letters from Mom, and basically survived.

When I arrived I was twenty pounds overweight, couldn't do a single "Marine Corps" pull-up, and could only do about ten sit-ups. When I graduated ten weeks later I was twenty pounds lighter, could do twenty pull-ups and forty push-ups. Mission accomplished, for both me and the Corps.

15

From: Paden Waldruff
Date: October 31, 2007
To: Robert H. Waldruff

RW: Ask all the questions you want no matter how trivial you may think they are. This may be your only chance and I'm fascinated by them.

PW: I will; thank you for indulging me. We'll have to get back to the politics at some point. I thought I had a really clear picture of your views, but since we've been writing, I am not so sure.

RW: Yes, we left on the journey sometime in the middle of November, with Mom and me heading east in our brand-spanking-new Ford Fairlane station wagon.

PW: Ouch! I laughed out loud when I read the word 'wagon.' You got stuck with a few wagons during your responsible-father days. It was interesting to me when BaBa Fegan and I went to he and Grans' house, at my request, he made an unconscious point of driving us over in his "small car," which was an old Porsche. Reclaiming his masculine identity, I think. Were you ever interested in motorcycles? You know I always have been, and I've gone far enough to get my license and to buy a bike. It was a darling 1972 Honda that has now been sold.

RW: During this trip we made a side trip to the Grand Canyon. Of course every time I see the Canyon, I'm in awe. This time was particularly beautiful as we headed back to the main road through a pine forest near Flagstaff as it was snowing. This just a few days after leaving the heat and smog of LA.

PW: I never knew you had such a travel bug. We stuck so much to tradition in our vacation paths, when Tucker and I were children. Do I need to see the Grand Canyon?

RW: General Fegan was selected for Brigadier General in September and he and Grans had left Washington for his new duty as Assistant Commander of the 2nd Marine Division stationed at Camp Lejeune, NC

PW: I would like to know and understand more about the pecking order and chain of command, so I can really understand the significance of what you just wrote about BaBa's career path. When BaBa Fegan and I were in his house, I saw a picture of BaBa's father, Joseph Charles Fegan. He was very handsome, and as we all know he gave his name to BaBa, Joseph Charles Fegan, Jr. Once, I asked his son, my uncle Joe, what people called BaBa, remembering the toggling for Uncle Joe between "Joe" and "Charlie." Uncle Joe said, "They called him 'The General.'" I am very interested in the history. And I am very interested in your family history. I feel like you and Mom didn't want us to ask.

RW: Mom and I saw Aunt Lou

PW: I wish that I could've known her as an adult. I wish that I could have a drink with Aunt Lou now, and get her perspective on being a woman in a man's world. I wish I could hear what she would say about the preceding sentence.

RW: and my college friend, Renny Barnes. We had a small party at his apartment in Arlington, and Mom and I spent the night there. The next day Mom dropped me off at OCS-Quantico. She headed to Camp Lejeune to stay with the parents until I, hopefully, completed OCS. Then she could join me while I attended The Basic School at Quantico.

PW: What is the difference between OCS and Basic?

So many thoughts. As you know, when you took me for my interview at Washington and Lee, I was mesmerized by VMI. I think my attraction was the pure competition, the emphasis in my naive belief was on the word "pure." But with an equal emphasis on my competitive nature. You gave that to me; genetically encrypted. I had a seminal dustup with Bill Massie, my UVA friend, when we watched a movie in which the Coach was telling the athlete that he needed to feel contempt for his opponent during every race. The athlete totally folded, because he didn't have that sentiment. I identified with Coach, because I felt that every time I competed. Bill identified with the broken athlete.

But the additional layer of the military that I now understand— it isn't a meritocracy. It is a political machine; internally most importantly. And what is also genetically encrypted in me is that I hate to be told what to do. I can get with the program when I totally agree; but other than that, no. So I can't imagine the conflicts that were going through your exhausted mind when you were stuffed into the barracks.

Can't wait to hear more.

16

From: Robert H. Waldruff
Date: November 28, 2007
To: Paden Waldruff

Paden,

Interesting that our correspondence has confused you on my political preferences. I'm a fiscal conservative and a libertarian on most social issues. And a DEDICATED believer that less government is better government.

No, I've never had an interest in motorcycles. I've ridden on a few but received no special feeling. I think a Vespa is about as far as I want to go.

Your Uncle Joe is an interesting guy. He's a lot like his sister (your mom), with a strong desire to please. He's very much a people person. I don't think he's got a mean bone in his body. He hates confrontation and politics. He's a really good guy, and totally devoted to his family. Not very complicated.

Back in the day, I loved to travel—my Venezuela excursions with Percy, and Jamaica, to give examples. During your childhood the beach was a family event, and seemed to please everyone without a lot of hassle. Don't forget we took you both to Spain. The Grand Canyon is a must-see. It really puts man and nature into perspective. It is awesome, and humbling.

The Marines have two categories, Officers & Enlisted (non-officers). The career path of an officer takes him through several ranks. That's assuming he stays in the Corps and gets promoted; it's not automatic. When a candidate successfully completes OCS (again, not guaranteed), he receives a commission into the Officer Corps and is awarded the rank of 2nd Lieutenant. About two years later, he is promoted to 1st Lieutenant. After another two to three years, he's promoted to Captain. I was a Captain when I retired.

These promotions are pretty much automatic, and this is when one decides to leave the Corps or pursue it as a career. After about four to five years as a Captain, one is promoted to Major. This is where the weaning begins. After six to seven years, one is promoted to Lieutenant Colonel; it gets more competitive, and more careers end there. Your Uncle Joe retired as a Lieutenant Colonel. In order to retire with full benefits, one must serve at least twenty years. I think Joe retired almost immediately after he went over twenty years. I was retired with full benefits having been deemed disabled to serve.

The next promotion occurs about six to seven years later, and is the rank of Colonel (known as a "full Colonel", not a Lt. Colonel). A lot of Lt. Colonels never get promoted. You have to remember that the Corps, compared to the other branches, is quite small. So a Colonel in the Corps is a lot harder to achieve than say in the Army. The next promotion is Brigadier General (the General Corps), and is quite selective. General Fegan was concerned about his chances due to his physical disabilities, caused by his wounds received in the Korean War.

Being a General in all branches (Admiral in the Navy) is quite an exclusive club, and quite a career achievement (like making partner at Price Waterhouse). A lot of good soldiers don't make the cut. A Brig. Gen. is awarded one star. The next promotion is a two-star or Major General, and occurs usually after three to four years. The politics from Lt. Colonel on are quite important, and obviously your grandfather was accomplished. After two to three years, one is awarded three stars and the rank of Lt. General.

This was BaBa's rank when he retired. There are only about ten Lt. Generals in the whole Corps—quite an accomplishment. The next and final rank is four stars, and the rank of General. In General Fegan's day the Corps had only two Generals: the Commandant and Assistant Commandant of the Marine Corps. General Fegan was a runner-up in being named Commandant.

Hope this helps. Thus, when General Fegan was sent to Camp Lejeune, he was just promoted from Colonel to Brig. General. It was his first assignment as a General, and he was one of only four Generals stationed at Camp Lejeune. So, the Sergeants instructing me at OCS knew my father-in-law was a General. What this meant, I'm still not sure. I know I wasn't granted special privileges. I'm pretty sure they continued doing their jobs as professionals.

I don't know much about Mom's grandparents, and as a matter of fact I don't know much about my grandparents. My father's mother, Lydia, was known to all of us as "Tootsie." She was around while I was growing up, as she divorced my father's father and became sort of a ward of the family. She worked at Marshall Field's Department store in downtown Chicago. She lived in a small two-room apartment, on the South Side of Chicago, which we visited often. She never drove a car, and probably never had a driver's license.

She was always with us and/or the Smiths on all the holidays, and she occasionally would babysit us. We grew up thinking she was pretty mean. When she retired she moved in with Lou and Mary, and would rotate spending time with us and time with Aunt Emmy. She caused a lot of friction for Lou with Mary. Lou felt dedicated and obligated. Since she had no family, she felt it wasn't fair to ask John or Emmy to house her.

I don't remember ever having spent time with her former husband, my paternal grandfather, Roy Lawrence Waldruff. I've seen pictures, but my father never talked about him. Word was that he lost all his money, which was invested in grain futures when the stock market crashed in 1929, and became an alcoholic. Prior to the loss. I believe he was pretty wealthy, and the Waldruffs were well known in the small farming community of Chrisman, Illinois.

His brother, Bob, lived in Chicago. Bob committed suicide

through carbon monoxide poisoning, from his car in his garage. Again, my father never talked about Bob. All I know of him is from Aunt Lou's story that her brother Bob ran up some serious gambling debts with some tough folks in Chicago. In an act of desperation, he embezzled money from his employer. When that was discovered, it made him so ashamed and desperate that he felt his only choice was to end his life. Lou told me my father was devastated. He had always looked up to his older brother, my namesake, and probably never reconciled this in his life.

Whew. Your paternal grandfather was a product of a broken home, and his older brother committed suicide, when he was a 17-year-old starting a new life on the South Side of Chicago. They lived in Hyde Park, in the shadows of the University of Chicago. He graduated from Hyde Park High School, having started high school in a fifty-student school in Chrisman, Illinois. This was when he met my mother, who was living in Chicago. There had been domestic trauma in her home life, caused by her abusive father who apparently beat his children often.

Sure you want to hear more? I've never purposely not talked about my family. I guess I didn't feel you were that interested. Besides, I thought this was about Vietnam? We can continue this family history discussion later, and I will be happy to fill you in on Aunt Lou, my second mother!

OCS (Officer Candidates School) is a ten-week program to indoctrinate recruits into the Marine Corps Officer traditions. It is both physical and mental, while at the same time it evaluates each individual to determine whether or not he is Marine Officer material. Those deemed unfit are dropped from OCS, and never become Marine Officers.

The Basic School, which is also at Quantico VA, is a twenty-one-week training program for recently graduated officers from OCS. All the students are newly commissioned 2nd Lieutenants. They don't know squat about being a Marine officer. The mission of The Basic School is to train and indoctrinate newly commissioned officers on how to be an Officer of Marines. It is a totally different atmosphere than OCS. There's no harassment, a lot of classroom time, and plenty of field exercises. There is a lot of night patrolling, ambush simulations, weapon firing, classes on how to throw hand grenades, etc. Married types got to live with their wives off base. They could go home most nights, unless there was a night exercise, and most weekends. It was actually an enjoyable experience, unlike OCS.

17

From: Paden Waldruff
Date: November 28, 2007
To: Robert H. Waldruff

Dear Dad:

Thank you so much. I am not being facetious when I say that I am hanging on every word you write.

So I definitely do follow directly in your footsteps with respect to politics. Though to be honest, the small (deceptively small) thing I would need to remove would be the word "most" from what you've laid out.

I would like to continue the family history lesson, and to hear about your second mother. I hate it when people make movie references, but here I go. There was a line in one of the Indiana Jones movies when Sean Connery was talking to Harrison Ford about his childhood. Apparently Dad (Sean) wasn't so into the kid thing. Sean tells Harrison, "You left home right when you got interesting."

I know Lou wasn't into the kid thing. I get her point; children can be tedious. But I've often thought about her. And remembered her symbolically when my entire apartment in Norfolk was furnished with her things. We lost Aunt Lou at the exact age for me when I could have actually had a conversation with her that might have piqued her interest. I honestly can't imagine what she would have bestowed upon me in terms of stories, history, and opinions.

I would also like to get back to the task at hand. The context you have provided helps a lot.

So you graduated after ten weeks of insanely intense physical activity. What next? Was there a graduation ceremony? If yes, how did you feel about it?

18

From: Paden Waldruff
Date: November 28, 2007
To: Robert H. Waldruff

Dear Dad:

I think I end up talking about my roots more than most people because of my name. It is an easy ice-breaker question for people to pose to me. I have always said I am Irish. That was my thinking of the Fegans; I was surprised when you told me Grans was Scottish. And also German. So am I right about my paternal heritage when I say German?

19

From: Robert H. Waldruff

Date: January 9, 2008

To: Paden Waldruff

Paden,

Aunt Lou was very special to me and our family. She liked to act as though she was tough. In a lot of ways she was, particularly competing as a woman in a truly man's world circa 1945-1970. But she really was a softy. She was proud of you and Tucker. She never stopped bragging to people how you, our daughter, was going to the University of Virginia. That bastion of male education! I truly think, as proud as she was that I went to UVA, I think she was prouder that you went—a woman thing, I believe. I'm sure she would have loved to have seen how you have matured as a young businesswoman, and would have greatly enjoyed talking to you.

She was a wise and smart woman. She had very good common sense and people smarts; she could tell a phony a mile away. She had a challenging adolescence, what with her parents' divorce and her brother's suicide. She assumed the leadership role for her brother John and sister Emily. That devotion and time-consuming task pretty much shut off any personal life. She always maintained communication with both siblings and their families. We all were truly an extension of her existence. I'm forever grateful that I got to benefit from her wisdom and her love.

As far as roots—paternally we are German, Welsh, and yes, Scottish. Maternally, as an indicator of how my mother shut off her parents from us, I couldn't for sure tell you her roots.

Before we leave OCS a couple additional pieces of info. Because the Marines organized us alphabetically, my physically closest classmates had last names beginning with W. Hence, my introduction to Bob Wood, aka Woody, who turned out to be a very close friend. Bob was what we called "gung-ho." My first recollections were of how squared-away and aware he seemed. As I eventually found out, he was actually being recycled through OCS. He originally began in February 1968. He went through six weeks, then broke his ankle. This could have gotten him a discharge. But because of his commitment and devotion to the cause, he rehabbed at the base hospital, healed, and started OCS all over again in my class. Think about it. He could have fulfilled his service obligation honorably, gone home to his wife, and gotten on with his life. But he chose not to. He's one of my heroes.

Here's another factoid to remember as this story unfolds. OCS had a test of leadership skills that included a staged area with an impossible to solve problem. For example, a small waterhole with only a rope and a six-foot two-by-four as props, and the mission was to get four people across the water. We were led to the area with our backs turned then told to face the test. One of our names was called out to be the team leader. Of course the problem was unsolvable, though we didn't know it at the time. The purpose was to teach that during combat, some plan was better than none. Well, my name got called and I pretty much did nothing as I tried to reason what the solution was. Soon, I was relieved as leader and another person was selected. Needless to say, I got severely graded and more or less flunked this important leadership test.

There was a formal graduation ceremony attended by Mom, Aunt Lou, and Renny Barnes. A lot of wives and parents attended, but it was too far for Grandma and Grandpa, and General Fegan must have had a conflict. It probably didn't seem like much of a ceremony for the guests, but it was a milestone day for the participants. We wore a Marine uniform for the first time, and got our 2nd Lieutenant gold bars. Also, just like in *An Officer and a Gentleman*, the first enlisted person who saluted us got a return salute and a dollar bill placed in his belt. Of course the enlisted person was our Platoon Sergeant. Pretty amazing feeling. Here was our mentor and all-knowing leader of the past ten weeks, effectively saying we were now his leader and superior. A very emotional and symbolic event. The four of us went to lunch, and that was pretty much it. We now had a three-day weekend to get an apartment and get set up. The Basic School began on a cold snowy Monday in February 1969.

20

From: Paden Waldruff

Date: January 20, 2008

To: Robert H. Waldruff

Dear Dad:

Thank you for writing about Aunt Lou, and thank you for telling me she was proud of me. It means a lot. As you know, Maureen chose to name our company after Lou and Mary. Aunt Lou was a pioneer and a road paver for my generation. I do wish I could sit down with her now and have a neat Scotch. I know you feel the same.

One quick aside that I just thought of—when I typed "Maureen" and "pioneer" in the same paragraph. When Maureen came to the desert with me, I dragged her very tired self to Pappy & Harriet's with the promise of one beer before we went home to bed. It is a famous underground steakhouse/bar for musicians (Emmy Lou Harris kind of musicians). I had been dying to check it out. It was packed. Couples in their sixties dancing, early twenty-something kids trying painfully to look cool, and Marines keeping to themselves.

We sat at the bar, right next to a table of twelve Marines. I assume they were Marines; they were in civilian clothes, but their hair was definitely high-and-tight. I felt strangely proud as I observed them. I've been consistently fascinated by the noble behavior of the desert Marines. I am sure I have a fascination with the myth. And I also noticed that the only storefronts in 29 Palms were haircuts, tattoos, and "massages." But I will say, every Marine I've seen has made me proud of my country.

When you mention Robert Wood being gung-ho, and that you met him when he was re-entering OCS after an injury, it makes me think of the book you and I discussed recently about Marines at Parris Island. It reminds me that he was in a challenging position when he re-entered. And it reminds me of the day our family went to the Vietnam War Memorial for the first time.

About the impossible leadership challenge you faced in training— I know I would have frozen.

I am (as always) on the edge of my seat. You had three days to find an apartment after graduation? You and Mom? Was Basic School in Lejeune?

Love,

P

21

From: Robert H. Waldruff

Date: January 25, 2008

To: Paden Waldruff

Paden,

You should feel pride when you see the Marines, not that the Army, Navy, and Air Force don't deserve it as well. It's not easy to be one of "us," and it isn't a journey for everyone.

The Marine Basic School was also at Quantico, about four miles from OCS. It was a twenty-two-week school that had probably 600 to 700 2nd Lieutenants in training. The mission was to instruct us on various facets of being a Marine officer. The single guys lived at O'Bannon Hall, a three-story building with dorm-type rooms. Each room had its own bathroom, so no more communal living. The married-types lived off base in rented homes, or usually in apartment buildings. A popular location was an apartment complex in Woodbridge just off I-95. This is where Mom and I settled, as did Bob and Shirley Wood, and about five other couples. It was a fifteen-mile commute, and the six of us usually carpooled. We were home most nights and weekends, unless we had an overnight class.

The curriculum was a mix of classroom lectures and outdoor field exercises. We also spent a week at the rifle and pistol ranges, learning how to fire and care for our rifles and pistols. We were tested to "qualify", by being scored on how many bull's eye targets we hit. We had daily PT and five-mile runs. Since we were all now in pretty good shape, this was actually looked forward to. Uncle Joe got heat stroke on one of these runs, and passed out. This has led to what I think are some of his physical problems today. You can imagine the atmosphere. All instructors were Marine officers, many of whom had recently served in Vietnam. A bunch of young men getting more confident by the day, and convinced of our invincibility. The term for this in the Corps is that we were getting pretty "salty."

Camaraderie was in abundance. We were involved in field problems that taught us tactical solutions to battlefield situations. We were introduced to the "five paragraph order" (SMEAC). The Corps had an acronym for almost everything. In retrospect, the Corps realized our training was not really of much value in the Vietnam jungle-war environment. It was still based a lot on WWII and Korea tactics, i.e., had not been properly revamped for teaching how to fight a guerilla war.

Regardless, there was still a lot of instruction that was valuable. We learned how to fire all the Marine weaponry including grenades, hand-held rockets, mortars, etc. We learned about Viet Cong mines and how to detect and disarm them. We learned how to use a compass, and how to read terrain maps. We learned about communications on various equipment. It's amazing how far we've come in warfare technology since 1969. Our radios were this twenty-five-pound piece of equipment with an antenna carried on the back of the radio operator, and had a range of only about five miles.

Mom and I had a pretty normal social life. We hung out, of course, with other Marine couples. We went to the officers club, movies, restaurants, and of course went to see Lou and Mary.

I started Basic School in the snows of February and graduated in the heat and humidity of July. Our last exercise was spending two days on a troop landing ship off the coast of Norfolk. We conducted an amphibious landing on Virginia Beach, complete with climbing down the web ropes of the ship and getting into the landing boats. This whole OCS/Basic School experience is one of the reasons the Marine officer is unique. We have all shared the same training experience. None of the other services have this common training experience. There were eight branches (MOS— Mode of Service) we could ask to serve in. But regardless of where we ended up, as the Corps proudly states: All Marines are trained as infantry riflemen.

The week prior to our graduation we were assigned our MOS. I asked for artillery. The most popular MOS was infantry, and about seventy percent were assigned this MOS-03. The best and worst graduates ended up in infantry (needs of the Corps). A lot of 03s were getting killed, so if you had a low class ranking and requested a non-infantry MOS, chances were you would be denied and be assigned 03. I was gung-ho and all that, but a Marine infantry officer seemed a little too risky. I thought artillery would be safer, but would still give me a combat MOS. It turns out it wasn't all that safe.

Bob Wood and I and about fifteen other Lieutenants were assigned Artillery MOS-08. Our own General Fegan was the invited guest speaker at our graduation, after which we all headed for Camp Lejeune. It was time to get pregnant Mom and me packed for fifteen weeks of Artillery School at Fort Sill in Norman, Oklahoma.

22

From: Paden Waldruff
Date: February 2, 2008
To: Robert H. Waldruff

Dear Dad:

I have memories of Quantico. One has become kind of a metaphor and pops into my mind at the strangest moments. Do you remember how much Tucker and I loved goof balls? I remember BaBa's driveway being on a hill, and I remember Tucker and I standing there watching helplessly as our goof balls made these gigantic freedom bounces down the hill. Other things that pop quickly into my mind are running (probably right after getting out of the car) around the gigantic house with Tucker (and getting in trouble but is was worth it), Uncle Wiggly, insanely gigantic piles of Christmas presents, snooping around in the little house out back where someone who worked for BaBa obviously lived and then getting in trouble for it, feeling terrified when a gigantic, smiling black man came in one Christmas and wanted to pick me up, crossword puzzles, parakeets, cigars, *Family Affair* on TV, and Gran's buzzer under the dining room table. Do I remember correctly that one Thanksgiving she wouldn't let me leave the table filled with guests until I tried my pumpkin pie? And I do remember correctly that I did and then threw up? Her will vs. my will equaled me feeling completely embarrassed?

And Woodbridge—Uncle Joe lived there too, right? In a condo in a subdivision? Was that around the time he brought Jerry, the policewoman, to Richmond and she sat on the glassed-in porch with us? Tucker and I thought she was AWESOME.

So you and Mom were in Woodbridge for twenty-two months. Everything I've ever read about the Marines speaks to the pride factor that all Marines are riflemen. And that was a long, intense period of time for all of you to get very close to each other.

And the General spoke at your graduation? Was he a good speaker? What was that like for you? What did your peers think of that? Did they rib you, or would that not be kosher?

And you and Bob Wood became MOS-08. I am following along here with a growing knot in my stomach. For the record, I frequently have at least a touch of a knot in my stomach, and it means risk/excitement/fear.

You and Mom lived in Oklahoma for fifteen weeks? Really? I never knew that.

Please continue as soon as you find yourself with a moment.

Love,

P

23

From: Robert H. Waldruff

Date: February 21, 2008

To: Paden Waldruff

Paden,

Yes, that was quite a castle Gen. and Mrs. Fegan lived in at Quantico. BaBa got command right after he got his third star to become a Lieutenant General. Don't remember the throwing up pumpkin pie episode, but sounds like something you would be involved in.

Yes, Uncle Joe lived at Woodbridge. He was attending Amphibious Warfare School (AWS), an important school for career Marines. That is where he met Jeanette.

The twenty-two weeks of The Basic School (TBS) did not seem long. It was intense, but mostly interesting. And of course, in the back of every mind (Marines and wives) was our date with destiny 7,000 miles away in a tiny, humid, and dangerous country. Individually and collectively, we didn't dwell on this obvious unavoidable fact facing our future. The instructors only mentioned Vietnam when their experience reinforced a teaching point. Of course, being young, indestructible, and Marine Officers, we never thought we would be harmed. Most of us (not all) thought it would be a thrilling adventure.

Before I move beyond TBS and OCS, I'll reiterate what a fabulous job the Marines do at training. In eight months they got me right off the University of Chicago campus, never having fired a weapon of any sort, and got me mentally, physically, technically, and emotionally ready to lead men in combat. Pretty remarkable. And, most of my peers were like me, not superhuman physical studs. Training is probably what the Corps does best.

I'm reading a book by a Marine who served in Korea called, *Why Marines Fight*, which concludes that the answer is the shared experience of TBS. We don't do it to kill the enemy, we do it to not let down our fellow Marines and/or disgrace the legacy of all Marines who preceded us. Sounds corny, but I agree; it's what makes Marines unique in the world.

BaBa's speech was straight from the book (he always took his Marine responsibilities seriously), and I felt special. We 2nd Lieutenants were impressed by Generals, and that my father-in-law was one made me a somebody in my class.

Bob Wood and pregnant wife, Shirley, left for his home in Arlington TX, and I and pregnant wife, Mom, left for the Fegan's quarters in Camp Lejeune. We met again in ten days in Lawton, OK, home of the Army's Fort Sill Artillery Base. The infantry officers graduated from TBS, training completed, and took off for assignments in the FMFPAC (Fleet Marine Force—Pacific), i.e. the real thing.

We artillery types, trained in infantry, had to learn about artillery. We Marines, same as all Army artillery types, were trained at Fort Sill. Marines didn't have the budget or facilities needed for training. It was at Sill that we Marines started to appreciate our Quantico training as we realized our superiority over the Army 2nd Lieutenants was not just braggadocio, but truth.

Our class was seventy to eighty 2nd Lieutenants, of which about fifteen were Marines. A lot of the Army types were right off the college ROTC campus with no actual field training. Needless to say, we Marines excelled at all the field problems, agitating the Army instructors. And the harder they tried to trip us up, the more motivated we became to excel.

Mom and I arrived in Lawton on July 15, 1969, and it was over 100 degrees every day for the next sixty days. Mom was getting bigger each day. After much searching, we rented a three-bedroom rancher with an awful cigarette odor but air conditioned. We Marines hung together and strengthened our Quantico bonds.

The next installment tells you more about my friend, Bob Wood, and more about our Lawton experiences as we marched to our fate.

24

From: Paden Waldruff
Date: March 20, 2008
To: Robert H. Waldruff

Dear Dad:

One housekeeping item. I didn't get your resend either; so odd. I am ready for the next installment. Two thoughts I had while reading my current text.

1. I don't think the sentiment you shared from *Why Marines Fight* is corny at all. I have heard the theme of Marines protecting each other and the Corps repeated many times. I find it brilliant, and it makes perfect sense to me. I have kind of a chicken and egg thought in my mind. Did the Marines set out to create a branch that instilled these values (which are subjective; can't force subjective) or did they set out to train the best infantry possible and the subjective values were the result?

2. The last line of your email told me that you are getting ready to tell me more about your friendship with Bob Wood. You referenced him in the body of the email, and I wondered while I was reading as I have wondered my whole life about him.

You are an extremely strong person. You have kept your own counsel in life. You take risks, and you stand by all of your successes and failures. I can't tell you how much I respect you. My guess would be that it isn't your choice to keep your own counsel. But the facts are that your profile is rare: an extreme risk-taker who is extremely responsible.

So I remember two moments in my formative years at 101 Gaymont when your resolve was tested. I can't remember which came first, but there were only two in eighteen years.

1. When I was in the midst of a dust-up with you in the basement about spending the night with Liz Orsi. Her mother was a divorcée and I was dying to get over there with her sister in charge. You were saying no and we were arguing. Then suddenly you got a phone call that your father had died. You ran up the basement stairs and my heart broke.

2. When we went to the Vietnam War Memorial with Aunt Lou and Mom. When you found Bob Wood's name, Lou took us kids aside, and my heart broke again.

25

From: Paden Waldruff
Date: April 23, 2008
To: Robert H. Waldruff

Dear Dad,

Lately I've taken to watching fictional portrayals of the Vietnam War and the current Iraq War (mixed in with a lot of other things when I just want to "chill.")

I must say, I am surprised by how many TV series there are on both wars, and the portrayal of each war is astoundingly different.

I know there is a lot going on, but I am looking forward to my next installment from you.

XO,
P

26

From: Robert H. Waldruff

Date: May 8, 2008

To: Paden Waldruff

Paden,

Joe did not meet Jeanette at Quantico; he met her in San Diego. Don't know what I was thinking.

Based on my experience, I think it's virtually impossible to accurately portray war in a movie. But, if there is an effort to be factual, I do think one can learn some things by watching combat movies. The problem is Hollywood always has an anti-war slant.

You've once again asked a thought-provoking question re "chicken or egg." The Marine Corps was founded at Tun Tavern in Philadelphia on November 10, 1775, by a group of young men. How the esprit grew and became the fabric of being a Marine probably began on this day and was passed on to each new member. I think the volunteer aspect has also attracted a more dedicated person than being drafted into one of the other services. Plus, I think the Marine Corps early on became great at self-promotion, and started believing their own propaganda. One of the great Marine legends is the story of Dan Daly at Belleau Woods in WWI. Daly went on to be awarded two Medals of Honor. At Belleau Woods the Marines were pinned down and there was an open field between them and the Germans. The legend has it that Daly stood up, faced the German guns, and yelled to Marines to get up and charge by saying "Come on you sons of bitches; you want to live forever?" You can well imagine the roar of 200 new 2nd Lieutenants when we first heard this story!

Bob Wood was the middle child of three boys, was born and raised in Ft. Worth, TX. He graduated from the University of Oklahoma, married Shirley, and worked as a petroleum salesman in Los Angeles. He got drafted, and like me chose to become a Marine. He was about five foot ten and strong as an ox. He was not an intellectual, but smart enough, somewhat like David Bigger. What you saw was what you got—no B.S. Shirley was just a plain old gal who truly loved Bob.

As I mentioned earlier, Bob broke his ankle at OCS and could have gotten a medical discharge. He refused; he wanted to serve his country. He spent seven months in rehab, and joined my class when he started OCS over. He was a lead-by-example guy, and finished number one in our OCS class. I didn't really know him in OCS except to admire his leadership, and his excellence at meeting the physical demands of OCS. It wasn't really an environment conducive to exploring the personalities of other people.

Our friendship flourished at TBS, as he and Shirley lived in our apartment complex in Woodbridge. Mom and Shirley spent a lot of time together too. Shirley was pregnant when we met her, and of course Mom became pregnant while at Woodbridge. So the four of us had a whole lot in common. We were young, dedicated to what we were doing, and had a lot of fun times together. When we got to Fort Sill (Bob also chose Artillery as his MOS) we bonded even more. Almost every evening Bob and I would jog five miles in the extreme heat of Oklahoma. We ate lunch together almost every day and were in class together all day long. Their daughter, Lisa, was born at Sill and Mom and I were the first ones to see her.

Bob and I talked about the Marines and our shared experience, and both were eager to get the ultimate test and get orders to Vietnam. After all, what good was all of this training without testing ourselves in combat? We spent all our time with the other Marines in our class, had a lot of cook-outs, beer busts, etc. A favorite memory was a cook-out we had at our house. Bob brought his homemade ice-cream maker, and we made fresh ice cream while watching Neil Armstrong land on the moon. Now, I don't know what the wives talked about re the next phase of our Marine Corps lives. I'd have to ask Mom. As I've aged, my sense is that the pressure and fear was much worse for the wives. We were headed for adventure; they were headed for separation, worry, and the unknown.

The Marine Corps had two divisions in Vietnam while we were at Sill. The 3rd Marine Division was deployed up by the DMZ, and the 1st Marine Division was deployed around Da Nang and the An Hoa Basin. Either one was fine with us, just so we got orders to Vietnam. We were to receive our orders prior to our graduation in October. But then in September Nixon announced the 3rd Marine Division was leaving Vietnam and re-deploying to Okinawa. When we got our orders, I was assigned to the 3rd Marine Division in Okinawa. Woody got orders to the 1st Marine Division; he was going to Vietnam! I was envious of him, and I suspect Shirley was jealous of Mom. No one knew for sure, but it was pretty much assumed that those of us assigned to the 3rd Marine Division would probably never see Vietnam. We'd probably do thirteen months on Okinawa; worst of all worlds, a separation but no glory!

Our orders directed all of us to leave from Norton Air Base in San Francisco on November 7, 1969. This was almost exactly a year from when I started OCS. We went to Camp Lejeune, got Mom settled. We spent about a week there, then I left for L.A. to meet Woody and spend four days with Grandma and Grandpa. Then we'd fly up to San Francisco and our destiny.

When we left North Carolina, we got up early and drove in the rain to the Raleigh-Durham airport. Mom was six months pregnant, and the trip was filled with small talk. What would we name our first-born (didn't know the gender in those days), getting Mom an apartment, promise to write everyday, etc ... We never even got close to talking about any potential danger, and quite frankly were pretty sure I wouldn't be seeing danger! On parting, we had a long embrace and kiss. Mom never cried. I since learned that she cried like a baby all the way back to Lejeune. She's always been a trooper.

Bob met me in L.A. We saw the sights, and had dinners with the folks and John and Sandy. Of course, they all liked Woody. I started to notice a change in Bob; he was a tad more focused and serious. I'm sure the goodbye to Shirley and Lisa was sobering, knowing he would shortly be in Vietnam.

We met two other Marines at LAX, flew to Frisco, got a hotel room, and headed out for dinner and a few pops. About 11 p.m. the other two went back to the hotel, because we were to leave the hotel at 7 a.m. Bob and I closed the bar, and didn't get back to our hotel until 4 a.m. There's this picture somewhere of Woody standing on the bed of other two guys, waking them up while holding a fire hose that he had removed from its case in the hallway! We made our flight, but were hung-over all the way to Okinawa!

27

From: Paden Waldruff

Date: May 8, 2008

To: Robert H. Waldruff

Dear Dad:

No questions this time, though of course I've got a few. I'm just really wanting you to continue. I will be reading this email over a few more times tonight.

I must tell you one weird coincidence. I was sitting in the vet's office on Monday learning about Sam's situation. I knew I was talking to the owner of the practice, so I looked up at his name plate. It said "Bob Wood."

28

From: Robert H. Waldruff
Date: May 31, 2008
To: Paden Waldruff

Paden,

As we move forward, I thought a quick overview of what a Marine officer does in an artillery battery would give you better insight into my Vietnam experience.

An artillery regiment has three battalions, and each battalion has three batteries. Each battery has six howitzers, and each battery supports an infantry battalion. The concept is this: when an infantry battalion and its four companies are on an operation, when and if they need artillery to support their mission, the batteries are called upon to fire their guns.

The way the battery knows where to fire its artillery rounds is this: each infantry company has a Lieutenant from the battery on the ground with the infantry company. He is a forward observer (FO). If the infantry company is attacked and/or needs artillery support to fight the enemy, this FO reads his compass and calls in the map-coordinates of the target to the battery.

The battery is set up several miles away, usually in a safe and fortified position. The battery adjusts the angle of its guns to fire rounds on the target, and then fires. Usually the first rounds are not right on the target. The FO would then adjust the rounds by calling in new coordinates based on where the rounds landed. This procedure is continued until the rounds are on target. Then the FO tells the battery to Fire For Effect (FFE). They "bring it on," and hopefully destroy and obliterate the target, be it man or material.

Obviously, being an FO is quite dangerous as he is right out with the grunts engaging the enemy. The enemy knows who he is and targets him for death, because without him the infantry company is a lot less threatening. FOs are always the new guys assigned to the battery.

Identifying targets on a map with a compass is not easy and takes a lot of practice. Also, the technique of adjusting the fire on the target takes a lot of practice. The better someone is at reading a map and adjusting the coordinates, the faster the rounds can be brought on target.

Fort Sill is in the middle of hundreds of miles of flat terrain and a perfect location to practice calling in fire. This is what we primarily did for our eighteen weeks at Sill. We did it from small aircraft, from bunkers, from buildings, from foxholes, at night, and during daylight. Practice, practice, practice. I actually got pretty good at this and finished 10th in my class.

29

From: Paden Waldruff

Date: May 31, 2008

To: Robert H. Waldruff

Dear Dad:

Thank you for taking the time to explain that. I find it utterly fascinating. I am able to find it fascinating because it is information about strategy and not specifics about implementation. Implementation is what makes my palms sweat.

To give me an idea of scope, how many men are in an artillery regiment?

And a few clarification questions:

The three battalions are the grunts, out front and in the most danger, right? Marine Corps infantry? Is this what "enlisted" tends to mean? I need to tell you about a conversation I had on the train recently; I wished I knew, and was embarrassed that I don't know what "enlisted" means.

The FO is with the infantry battalions, right?

The words battery and company are interchangeable, right?

Two additional thoughts:

From everything I have read about the Vietnam War, I would guess that it would be really difficult to put the artillery regiment structure into place. How could you really figure out who the enemy was? I would guess that there were many moments for many soldiers when decisions were thrust upon them.

30

From: Robert H. Waldruff

Date: June 9, 2008

To: Paden Waldruff

Paden,

Let's finish up your questions of Marine unit structure. There are about 1,200 Marines in an artillery or infantry battalion. Infantry are what, in today's vernacular, boots on the ground. They are frequently called grunts and out front in the most danger. This is why being an FO is special being with the grunts, out front. Grunts are a hard bunch to impress, understandably, and when they accept an FO as one of their own it's an honor.

Marines have the rank of either officer or enlisted, officers are senior to all enlisted and expected to lead. There are about 30-40 officers in a battalion. A Battery is to an Artillery Battalion what a Company is to an Infantry Battalion. The six howitzers are in a Battery that supports the Infantry Battalions.

You are correct, since there were no front lines, the Artillery had to be creative on placement of their howitzers. They were almost always on a hill, thus the reference earlier to so many Hills, strategically placed to support Grunt operations in a 360 radius. Oftentimes the artillery placement sacrificed security to be able to support the grunts; thus, lots of time they were overrun by the VC and NVA. Juicy targets!

Now, back to the flight to Okinawa.

The flight from Frisco to Okinawa is twenty-three hours and goes across the international dateline, i.e., today is tomorrow in Okinawa. Or is it yesterday? We stopped to refuel in Hawaii and Wake Island. Due to our condition, Bob and I slept most of the way. We arrived in Okinawa at night, and we all checked into barracks near the airfield. The next morning, Bob and the other Marines with orders to Vietnam were trucked off to a staging area. There they would get special shots, be issued jungle utilities and boots, and be given some indoctrination information. The rest of us were trucked off to Camp Hansen, our home for what we thought would be the next thirteen months. The Army, Air Force and Navy had twelve-month tours. The Marines, always trying to outdo the other services, required thirteen-month tours!

Camp Hansen was a pretty large base with a lot of barracks, mess halls, truck repair facilities, and other stuff. Outside the main gate, like at all Marine bases domestic and foreign, was a small town. This was Kin Village, comprised mostly of bars and whorehouses. We had a syphilis rate among the enlisted Marines of over fifty percent. They would get paid twice a month, and take their cash to town. There the girls were all dressed up waiting, and of course soon the Marines would be drunk and easy prey for a wily prostitute.

My first roommate was Harry Tower. You may remember he and his wife and two children came by our house several years ago. Back then, he was a bachelor, and kind of spacey.

Our daily routine was to have breakfast at the officers club, go to our battery, train, and exercise. We would all have dinner at the club, after which we would have some shooters at the bar. Fifty cents a drink. Several of us would go to Isakawa, a city about fifteen miles away. They had higher class bars than Kin Vil and Filipino singing groups mostly mimicking the Beatles. We would drink a few beers and get a cab back to Camp Hansen, go to bed, and start the whole boring routine over the next day.

After about a month, one night I went to bed around 10 p.m. and Harry went off to Kin Vil with some guys. He came back and I was asleep. He collapsed in the bathroom, and I found him on the floor the next morning. I thought he was hungover as he was groggy and incoherent. I put him in his bed, and went off to breakfast. When I came back I noticed he really looked strange. I called the MPs, who took him to the hospital in Naha, the capital city of Okinawa.

Seems Harry had an aneurysm of the brain, and was within an eyelash of death. It was around Christmas. The Marines flew his parents over, and we all prayed at the hospital. Harry started to improve and got to the point where it was safe to fly him home.

Long story short, Harry recovered to the point that he could complete his three-year obligation. He actually did another tour in Okinawa. A lucky man.

My next roommate was Ed Zeigler, a red-headed bachelor. Ed was a piece of work. He finished nine of the required ten years of divinity school to become an ordained priest, then instead quit and joined the Marines! I really liked Ed, and we had a lot of interesting conversations.

The time of your arrival was approaching, and I lived to get letters from Mom. She would tell all about what was going on and describe all the preparations for your arrival. Remember that in those days we did not know the gender, so we didn't know if we were having a daughter or son.

I wrote to General Fegan asking if he could intervene and get me orders to Vietnam. He refused, saying I had to follow proper channels starting with the CO of my battalion, a Colonel. I always figured General Fegan didn't want to interfere with destiny, and also open himself for criticism of favoritism. I spoke to the Colonel, and he forwarded my request up channels to the Inspector General. The IG gave me the same response given to many other Marines with the same request: Denied!

The battery I joined had several 1st Lieutenants who had served with this battery at Dong Ha, a very dangerous hilltop near the DMZ. They were a great bunch of guys including Bob Brown—he of four Purple Hearts! They took us under their wings, and the brotherhood continued.

Training in Okinawa was pretty difficult, as the locals didn't want artillery fire anywhere on the island. We were restricted to one training area, and could only "live fire" once a month. Thus, we were forced to do "dry drills."

All in all, Okinawa kind of sucked. Training was limited, I was away from Mom, I was pretty bored, and I couldn't get to Vietnam. It looked like it would be a long thirteen months. Christmas came and went—we all said it was the year without Christmas—and January 1970 rolled around. Little did I know what an eventful year it would be!

31

From: Paden Waldruff
Date: June 15, 2008
To: Robert H. Waldruff

As these emails progress, the sweatiness of my palms progresses as I read them. I know I got to grow up with you, so the suspense/fear factor is somewhat tempered. But I don't know your story, or the stories of the men who served beside you. The sweatiness of my palms is anxiousness, an excited heartbeat, and nervousness for you and everyone you grew to care about.

Okinawa sounds like a recipe for trouble. Young men, danger looming, foreign country, daily boredom, cash, cheap drinks, and available women ... Dear God.

Harry Tower—was he the father of the twins, the boy and girl that we went to dinner with at the Ground Round?. You asked for orders to Vietnam? I know I have no right to an opinion, and will never be in a position to find out, but, I think I would've done the same. Knowing what you now know, would you still have asked?

Please proceed whenever you have time.

32

From: Robert H. Waldruff

Date: June 19, 2008

To: Paden Waldruff

Paden,

I don't want to ruin the ending for you, but I do come home alive! Okinawa was a recipe for disaster. It made being an officer even more challenging, in that you had to keep the troops motivated. The challenge was made greater by the fact that a lot of the enlisted Marines had served in Vietnam. They had gotten bad attitudes and/or a chip on their shoulder, and they wanted to go home and be discharged. On Okinawa, they found the training exercises being led by untested 2nd Lieutenants—guys like me—totally worthless.

Harry Tower had a son and daughter; they came through Richmond and spent a couple hours at Gaymont. We went to the Ground Round with Jeff and Linda Schmitt and their two boys. I liked Jeff—he was a wild man from West Virginia. While we were together on Okinawa he was my regular partner on evening trips to Ishikawa. We would buy six bottles of beer at the Officers Club then get a cab. Halfway to town we would get the cab to stop so we could hide the beers in the sugar cane. On our way home, we would stop the cab, get the beers, and drink them while heading back to our rooms.

We will never know, but I believe you would have also asked to go to Vietnam for the same reasons. I didn't start this journey to end up in Okinawa. I wanted to be tested, and to see combat. No guts, no glory. Yes, I would still have asked, if I knew then what would happen later. I have no regrets. I could have done without the wounds, but they were part of the adventure. I believed then, and still do today, that America was right to be in Vietnam, and that it was my obligation to serve.

In January 1970, I was 25, and Bob Wood was 23. Okinawa was chilly in January, light jacket or sweater weather. Ed Zeigler bought an old used car from a Marine going back to the US, and we drove all over the island on weekends. We saw the "suicide cliffs." There, during WWII, the Japanese jumped to their deaths rather than be captured by US troops. They feared they would be tortured; this was propaganda fed them by their leaders. We saw all the little beach villages on both sides of the island, the mountain resorts of the Japanese vacationers, and most everything else. This broke up the monotony and made time go by.

The letters from Mom got more exciting as your arrival got nearer. Doctors said she and you were healthy. There's always that fear your child will be born with a mental and/or physical defect;

one is a little nervous.

February started with the information our Artillery Battery would deploy near Mt. Fuji for three months of cold-weather training. We were scheduled to depart on February 22, 1970. This was exciting news! We would be leaving Okinawa, going to the mainland of Japan, which I had never seen. And we would be stationed at a camp where we could conduct live-fire training exercises. This did, however, further indicate Lt. R. H. Waldruff would probably never get orders to the Republic of South Vietnam.

Around the 5th of February, Bob Wood showed up at Camp Hansen. Seems the Marines remaining in Vietnam were preparing to pull out completely over the next six to twelve months. They were sending some officers to Okinawa for Disembarkation School, training on how to organize the withdrawal of the Division. This seemed further proof that I was not going to Vietnam. I finally got real, and pretty much forgot about ever getting there. It was great seeing Bob. We traveled around in Zeigler's car, and heard a lot of war stories. I've still got pictures of the three of us at a beach.

Bob seemed to have aged and become weary of the adventure. I think he had now "been there done that," and simply wanted to get home. He told me so in private. We never had emotional heart to hearts, except this one time. He told me that he really missed Shirley and Lisa, and wanted to get home to them, to get on with the rest of his life as father and husband. I think this was one of the many reasons I took, and still take, his death so personally. I had the conversation with him that Shirley and Lisa should have had!

I still was jealous, but started to think maybe it wasn't all that bad that I would miss Vietnam. We didn't have the modern communication technology that exists today, e.g. cell phones. The communication modes were telegraphs, snail mail, and long distance telephone that cost an arm and a leg. We also had MARS, Military Air Relay Station. This was how you could talk to someone in the US on a military communication satellite network. There was a fifteen-second voice delay, and God knows how many people were listening in.

On February 17, 1970, I got word I would be receiving a MARS call from Mom. I believe it was early morning. I got in place, put the headphones on, and got some of the most exciting news I would ever receive. I was the father of a healthy beautiful girl named Eleanor Paden. Mother and child were both doing fine. Mom and I talked for a while, but not long. It was awkward, and it wasn't a private line. I couldn't wait to tell Woody! I still think it's an amazing coincidence that Bob was there with me at this time. I got pictures in the following days of this creature with a tuft of red hair. Grans attached a note saying she thought you had the potential to be beautiful. We were all relieved and excited.

On the 21st Bob and I went to Kin Vil, drank some beer, and saw the strip shows. We went to several whorehouses with me being the straight man, saying my friend just got here from Vietnam and wanted "some action." They would say "No problem, GI. $5 short time, $10 all night." I would say "Too much money, need to reduce price." They would say "Forget it GI. Payday soon." Meaning there would soon be plenty of Marines with lots of money willing to pay full price. We did this for about an hour, then went back to the Officers Club for a few pops.

We said goodbye, hoping we would be stationed together back in the US after our tours ended in the Pacific. That was the last time I would see Bob Wood alive.

The next day we went to White Beach, got our battery on the ship, and headed for Japan.

33

From: Paden Waldruff
Date: June 19, 2008
To: Robert H. Waldruff

Dear Dad:

God, I have this huge lump in my throat.

I know I keep saying this, but I simply cannot believe how young you were. It really smacked me in the face again when you said you were 25 and Bob Wood was 23.

And the dichotomy is intense.

On the one hand, I love your stories, the fact that you were maximizing your experience, and the guys you picked as friends. With each line you write, I can imagine myself there. I am loaded up with my two cents, and with the jokes I want to throw into the mix.

BUT, there is the other hand. And that brings me back to the lump in my throat.

Ready to proceed whenever you are.

34

From: Robert H. Waldruff
Date: June 20, 2008
To: Paden Waldruff

Paden,

Actually, Bob was 24. I know you keep dwelling on this age thing, I guess relating it to you and your generation. Let's not forget there are men and women today of these ages fighting and dying for our country, and each person has a story.

The sea voyage to Japan was interesting. We were on a Navy troop-hauler, along with an infantry company and assorted logistics personnel. All the 2nd Lieutenants could not sleep in the officer area due to lack of space. Instead we were housed in the bowels of the ship in the brig, eight of us stacked up in a room the size of a closet. We found out this ship had recently been used to transport some NVA POWs, and they were quarantined in this very brig. My hatred of the Navy, an old Marine tradition, began on this trip. All the Marines were treated as second-class citizens. Marines had to wait for chow until all the Navy types had eaten, had to clean up the ship for the lazy swabbies, etc ...

The trip was about three days through the Sea of Japan, and we arrived on Numazu Beach. We were greeted by a group of Japanese protesters, anti-US and anti-Vietnam War. It was not a very big group, rather a non-event. Seems there were not enough trucks to haul all the battery personnel to Fuji (about a fifty-mile trip) so a group of Marines had to stay overnight on the beach and I was put in charge. Luckily we had sleeping bags, as around 3 a.m. it started to snow! Here we were in a snowstorm, when four days earlier we were in the heat and humidity of Okinawa. Got to love the Marine Corps.

Next day we got settled in at the foot of Mt. Fuji. We were housed in tents kind of like the ones on the television show M*A*S*H. We really got to know each other. There were eight of us officers, six of whom had served with this battery in Vietnam. The training was intense but enjoyable. It was great learning from these officers, and they willingly and patiently brought me up to speed on serving in a combat artillery battery. Fuji is a beautiful mountain, once long ago an active volcano. It snowed often and was generally pretty chilly at around 40 degrees F.

We traveled almost every weekend throughout the country. They have bullet trains, making travel pretty convenient. We saw Tokyo, toured the site of the Olympics recently held there, went to the ancient capital, Kyoto, and visited the World's Fair which was in progress. We also went to a Marine-sponsored orphanage, as ambassadors of goodwill, and entertained the children with a hamburger cook-out. We visited several other large cities, including Yokasuka, which housed a large Navy base and hospital. Little did I know I would be back to this base and hospital for my 26th birthday.

During this time I had my second molar removed, compliments of the USMC, in an old quonset hut. In March I was promoted to 1st Lieutenant. It was no big deal, just a little more money. I received frequent progress-reports from Mom about herself and about you. I told General Fegan often that this was probably my most enjoyable time as a Marine. The training was challenging and rigorous, the morale of the troops was high, and there was a great camaraderie amongst the officers.

It was at Fuji that I met 1st Lieutenant Dennis Ryan, an Irish Catholic. He was a motor transport officer. "Motor T and out in three" was their motto (my friend Ed Zeigler was also Motor T). Dennis had a great sense of humor, was intelligent, and didn't take himself too seriously. He was another of my favorites. After I was wounded he heard through the grapevine that I had been killed. He wrote this long letter to Mom about how much he liked me, saying he hoped the rumor was false.

I have a lot of pictures of Japan, of myself, and of my fellow officers in Japan. These include the infamous one of me with my mustache (you can hardly see it), which I shaved after about four weeks. Japan is a small place with a lot of people, and everybody seemed quite polite and friendly. By now I was getting pretty darn good with my FO skills, and was getting fire on target pretty fast with accuracy. This would come in handy. We trained through April, and as spring arrived it started to warm up and the cold weather dissipated. Our training wrapped up, and we shipped back to Okinawa in early May.

When we got back to Okinawa, we heard President Nixon had made the decision to launch a major military operation into the "parrot's beak" section of Cambodia. This was hugely controversial back home. It was the first time the US would go to a neighboring country of Vietnam to kill the NVA in their sanctuaries. If we had done this throughout the war, such as invading the Ho Chi Minh Trail in Laos, a lot of historians think we would have defeated the NVA. Nixon knew time was running out with Congress and US public support, so he gambled that this bold action would cripple the North.

It was during a student protest of this Cambodian incursion that the National Guard shootings at Kent State took place. As you know a Guardsman shot at a group of protestors, killing two and wounding one. When we got word of this, the saying was "National Guard 2, Kent State 0." Because Nixon and the military were not sure of what would happen in Vietnam vis-a-vis casualties and enemy attacks, word went out that every officer on Okinawa who had not been to Vietnam was to get orders immediately to ship out and deploy to the Republic of South Vietnam!

Wow—I got my orders in a few days and was actually going

to Vietnam. The coolest thing was when I got my combat fatigues and combat jungle boots. That meant I was on my way. This turn of events happened so fast that I didn't have time to think about it much, but I was excited. We laughed about how I had just finished three months of cold weather training, and was now heading for the hot humid jungles of Vietnam. I was all set to head for the airbase and the overnight staging area for the flight to Vietnam when our Battalion Commander called me into his office about a telegram he had just received.

35

From: Paden Waldruff
Date: July 6, 2008
To: Robert H. Waldruff

Dear Dad:

I know I am fixated on the age thing. Part of the fixation is directly related to knowing there are male and female soldiers in harm's way as I type to you, Many of them are also in their late teens and early twenties.

While I definitely do not know how it feels to be a teenager, or in my early twenties, representing the United States Armed Forces in a hostile situation that also has a large boredom/down time component, I do know that we have very limited experience to draw from at that age. And I know the enemy on the ground is largely the same age. So my thought is that either instinct or training are ruling any confrontation. My hope is that our troops are ruled by training, but what about the other side? My fear is that an angry, untrained group of rogues from the opposing side could unravel the best training for our soldiers in a heated, unexpected interaction.

And of course, my heart breaks for young soldiers with children.

Here I've spent thirty minutes typing on this one topic. Every line of your emails is packed with so much information.

Three days on the sea getting your chops busted by Navy guys? Sleeping in a room with eight other guys? My nose is wrinkling. Plus logistics. So many people I meet seem to have such a lack of understanding of the difficulty/reality of logistics in any situation. So, after the trip to Japan, you got left on the beach and in charge. And there was a protest when you landed. And it was snowing. Dear God.

And once again, I am thrilled and inspired by the way you chose to spend and interpret your time at Mt. Fuji and in Japan. Life is so short and we only get one chance, so why not take every moment and try to shoot the moon?

I would be curious to hear more about what the six officers who had served already in Vietnam taught you.

I do not know about Parrot's Beak or very much about Nixon's acumen as Commander in Chief. But, from all the documentaries I've watched, I do have the deep impression that the NVA was swarming all over Cambodia and Laos. The histories of the three countries are so intertwined. And Pol Pot's growing power with the Khmer Rouge during this time. It truly startles me that the small numbers of people in my generation who know that Laos and Cambodia were a huge part of the Vietnam War believe that Cambodia was a gentle agrarian country that got trampled by the

US. How is it that Pol Pot and Ho Chi Minh are forgotten, and the US as imperialists is remembered in our country? I know. I know the answer.

So, you were suited up and ready to go. What was the telegram?

36

From: Robert H. Waldruff

Date: July 17, 2008

To: Paden Waldruff

Paden:

You've not asked a dumb question yet. As a matter of fact, I've enjoyed your inquiries and thought-provoking feedback.

As to your worry about soldiers unraveling on the field of battle, I don't know if this relates to the so-called US atrocities like My Lai and/or fear for US soldiers from enemy atrocities. All I can say is that the only way to prevent this behavior is discipline, not that every leader possesses this and/or enforces it. This is a big reason behind Marine training starting with the first haircut at OCS.

The battlefield gets quite chaotic, and without leadership and discipline it would quickly turn into a mob scene. The winners on the field of battle are the best trained, best equipped, and best disciplined. The NVA and VC, by the way, were very courageous, dedicated, disciplined fighters. As for the terrorists, I can't speak to their discipline, but I'll bet it's better than you think.

The six officers with Vietnam experience didn't give us "rules to live by" per se, but reinforced our confidence and belief that our training was sound, and that Vietnam was not 24/7 action and danger. They had good attitudes, and didn't treat us as inferiors because of our lack of combat. As a matter of fact, they were pretty humble about their combat experiences. I've noticed many times that men who have combat experiences are very humble (because it's really not a glorious experience).

The US did not create the "killing fields" of Cambodia; they were created by Khmer Rouge Communists with North Vietnamese support after we deserted South Vietnam. This fact the liberal anti-war crowd, to this day, will not discuss relative to their "great victory" over the US government.

The rest of my story is based on a lot of recalled events and facts that I probably don't have completely accurate due to a fading memory, and the fact that a lot of information I received from third parties such as my wounding episode, etc. I'll give it my best, and you keep asking questions as that's your part of our bargain. Here goes!

The Colonel told me the Marine Corps had received a request from the Red Cross that I escort home the body of a fallen Marine, namely, First Lieutenant Robert T. Wood. It was like I didn't hear him; a kaleidoscope of feeling—emotion, fear, sorrow, and helplessness—splashed my psyche all at once. Bob Wood, dead. I knew I had to go, and I got concerned again about my destiny with Vietnam. Would this delay or cancel my orders? The Colonel assured me no, and instructed me to get in touch with the Red Cross via telephone. The Marine Corps would issue me temporary orders to perform escort duty.

I immediately called the Red Cross (with time zones and datelines, I probably had to wait until late night). They informed me that Shirley Wood had made the request, and that I needed to coordinate the funeral with her.

I then called Shirley, who I think cried, begging me to do this for her. She didn't have to plead; I would do ANYTHING I could for Shirley and Lisa. We talked a little longer and I promised her I would bring Bob home safely.

Neither Mom nor I remember how we coordinated her trip with you to meet me at Grandma and Grandpa's in LA after the funeral. I didn't call anyone, and Mom doesn't remember sending any telegrams. We think maybe BaBa intervened and pulled some strings. Regardless, the plan was for me to go from Okinawa to Arlington, TX, for the funeral, then go to LA to meet you and Mom for some R & R, then return to Okinawa, and then on to Vietnam. You both would go to Arlington, TX, to spend some time with Shirley and Lisa, then return home to Jacksonville, NC.

It's interesting that you mentioned the importance of logistics as a key to execution of any plan. The Marine Corps always emphasized logistics as a key to any successful battle plan. The logistics of returning Bob to his final resting place were all set. Next phase—execution.

Bob was killed around midnight of May 13, 1970. He was performing duties as an artillery forward observer at Firebase Ryder in the Que Son Mountains. He was coordinating an artillery attack on NVA troops moving through the Que Son Valley during a rainstorm in the middle of the night, thinking their movement would not be noticed.

Seems the Marines had started using IODs (integrated observation devices), set up in tall wooden towers. These were essentially a high-powered telescope with night-vision capabilities. The towers were sixty to eighty feet high. For some reason Bob wasn't using standard field radio equipment with an antenna powered by battery, but instead was using a landline phone with the line going down the tower to the land below. Apparently lightning hit the line, traveled up to the phone in Bob's ear, and electrocuted him. He probably did not feel a thing.

I often wondered if Woody's family, knowing his death was caused by an act of nature and not enemy fire, made them feel his death even more meaningless. All I know is that he died performing his duty as a brave Marine in a combat situation.

I got my orders and headed for Kadena Air Force base near Naha, Okinawa. I got on the first available plane leaving Naha for Travis AFB outside San Francisco, the same Travis AFB that Woody and I left seven months earlier with a hangover. I was to meet and receive his casket at Treasure Island Naval Base, a beautiful facility at the foot of the Golden Gate Bridge. The plane was a C-141 cargo transport. I hopped in, noting that there was a cockpit in the front, and the rest of the plane was a huge open space filled with equipment like generators, trucks, etc. and four little canvas swing seats, to be my home for the next fifteen hours.

37

From: Paden Waldruff
Date: July 19, 2008
To Robert H. Waldruff

Oh God, I was assuming the telegram was informing you that
you had a healthy wife and child. My assumption could not have
been more wrong, a lesson I learn over and over in a positive and
negative way. Never make assumptions about how life turns out.
Very painful to read; a fallen Marine. Makes me feel sick.

Two thoughts:

1. I don't quite know how to articulate this first one. I'd bet
I could do it in four words, a few days from now. It feels to me
that being a soldier in a combat zone is like life on steroids. Now,
before you roll your eyes and think, "Duh! That's about as stupid
as asking what happens when you try to put gas into a full tank,"
bear with me. I'm thinking past the obvious.

a. In a way, my guess is that being a soldier in combat becomes
like any other job (the Vietnam draft makes a huge difference, but
work with me)—you get the gist of what you are supposed to do
each day and you do it. Things become normal, yet the unexpected

happens every day, and the most adaptive soldier quickly adjusts, just like any job. Some days you are really focused and paying attention, some days you aren't. Some days you get your job, some days you think it's stupid, some days you make mistakes. The steroids part comes from the fact that any oversight or miscalculation or actual mistake has very different consequences in a war zone.

Just to be clear, I am in total agreement with you that Bob Wood died a hero, and I hope his family agrees. The above thoughts are spurred by the endless risks that combat entails.

b. I think Americans like me, who have never been a soldier at war, have this naïve sense that when you are deployed you are transported to some kind of bubble, and out of reality, and completely absorbed in the experience, so you can focus on your own safety and your mission. But, that's not true; even less so these days with email, etc. Life goes on for a soldier when he's doing his job, and he is a part of that life, meaning he is just as mindful of the ups and downs of his personal life as any businessman. But, a soldier is not a businessman.

I know I'm kind of babbling, like I said, I'm working on my point here; your story is making things less abstract and more personal.

2. On a completely different note, I realized early in my life how incredibly strong you are. Bold, chin out, driven, and VERY resilient. Every child should be fortunate enough to have a father with those traits. It translates into a sense of security, which

converts to confidence as life goes on. Plus, you are ridiculously smart. Intellectually, but even more so, street smart. And, on top of that, you are dedicated. You will go down fighting, to keep your word.

To interject myself into this story for a moment, we both know that when growing up in your house, my relationship with you was oftentimes adversarial. And yet there was a current of complete connection, especially when I needed you. You NEVER let me down (thank you).

Now that I'm 38, I can report from experience that you are quite rare, possibly unique. And as we work together on a regular basis, I'm oftentimes almost amused by the fact that I respectfully defer to you. This is something I've never done in my career (for better or worse), and something I didn't openly do when you were raising me.

So, when you refer to your devotion to your friend, Bob Wood, and when you said you would do ANYTHING for Shirley and Lisa, I know you MEANT it, and meant it for life. I almost can't bear the thought of the heaviness on your heart for his loss; and I do remember our first trip to the Vietnam War Memorial with Aunt Lou. Twice in my life I've seen you too hurt for me to bear: the night your father died, and the day Aunt Lou was explaining to Tucker and me what it meant when you found your friend Bob Wood's name on the Memorial.

So, you boarded the C-141. I will admit I have water in my eyes. What happened on the fifteen-hour flight?

38

From: Robert H. Waldruff
Date: July 23, 2008
To: Paden Waldruff

Paden,

I think you've done a pretty good job of understanding what a combat deployment is all about. It's human nature, I suppose, that under any circumstance we seek normalcy and routine. Living in a combat zone is no different. I guess a lot of people think it's 24/7 stress and fear; quite the contrary. Have you ever heard the saying "Combat is 90 percent boredom and 10 percent utter and sheer terror." I'd bet even being a POW was full of mostly daily routine, even if a routine a lot different than most are used to.

Now, I reiterate that my experience and knowledge are related and unique to me. Someone else may tell a totally different story. The other thing to remember, which is almost impossible to put in perspective, is that I'm telling this story after thirty-eight years of reflection and thought. This gives an obviously greatly altered account of my emotions and perspective on these events than I may have had as they occurred.

Slow down on the compliments! Besides, if I'm so smart how come I'm messing around with Darrel? Think about it. It is amazing how often we are totally in sync and on the same wavelength. I just told Mom this weekend that I bet Paden is doing stuff with/for me that she would never do for anyone else in a work environment.

I went back in a C-140; I don't know where I got the 141 from. You know I don't remember feeling a lot of grief and loss. I certainly didn't cry, except once at the funeral I got a little teary-eyed. I mean I certainly thought about it constantly. I also thought about what the visit/funeral would be like, what my role would be, and what was expected from Bob's family and Shirley and the Marine Corps. This was a lot bigger than just us participants. A lot of people would be scrutinizing my behavior vis-a-vis the tradition and reputation of the USMC.

The flight was extraordinarily uncomfortable. I had on my short-sleeve Marine Corps shirt and slacks, and the cargo-hold was very cold. I remember trying to curl up on a metal slab next to a huge generator to try to sleep. It was almost useless. The flight seemed to take forever, and I finally arrived at Travis AFB. I took a military transport to Treasure Island, and checked in at the Officers Quarters. Treasure Island was where Bob's remains had been delivered and were stored in the morgue. I spent the night, ate at the Officers Club, and felt very alone. The next morning I signed for Bob's casket and took possession and responsibility.

This whole escort thing was fairly unusual, as you can imagine the logistical nightmare if all families of fallen Marines in Vietnam requested escort from another Marine stationed in Vietnam. I mean the Corps could have said no. "We" were taken back to Travis and put on a cargo plane, and off we went to face the unknown. After landing in Dallas, I disembarked to the tarmac and waited for the casket. It was removed from the hull and put on the back of a pick-up truck sort of vehicle. I rode with him in the back of the truck with the American flag draped over the casket. I don't have any idea what people thought when they saw us driving across the airfield. We got to the terminal and the hearse from the funeral parlor met us. We put Bob in the back, I sat up front, and we drove to the funeral home in Arlington, TX.

I can't remember for sure, but I think Shirley met me and we drove to meet Bob's family. Bob was the middle of three boys. I guess his older brother was about 30, and the younger one was in high school. His mother and father looked absolutely devastated. We all engaged in some small talk, and I don't remember much. That night there was an open casket viewing at the funeral home. By this time I had caught up with the Marine Major sent from Dallas to instruct me on my duties. This night I was to stand behind the casket at parade rest while everyone paid their respects. I'll never forget the moment when Shirley got to the casket, looked in, and screamed "It's not him! It's not Bob!", then slumped over and cried hysterically. I can still hear her cry out. Bob's father was missing in action for the remainder of the funeral, including the ceremony the next day at the cemetery. I never saw him again.

The burial the next day included eulogies, prayers, and taps. A Marine guard unit carried him to the grave and lowered him down. I delivered the funeral flags to Shirley and Mrs. Wood. I handed each flag to the crying women, saying "The President, Marine Corps, and a grateful Nation thank you for your sacrifice." It is hardly enough, but that is the protocol. I stood up and saluted as the service ended. I teared-up, and immediately removed myself to a distance hoping no one would see. Later, in a letter, General Fegan said I received a good report from the major on how I handled the affair.

I felt tired and used-up.

39

From: Paden Waldruff

Date: July 23, 2008

To: Robert H. Waldruff

Dear Dad:

Jesus Christ. I am crying. I have the "luxury" of reading (not living) your experience in the privacy of my own home, so I can cry without letting anyone down or being judged. The image of Shirley and everything you went through to be a part of that image ... while you had your own personal life and concerns. Jesus Christ.

Are you familiar with the Myers-Briggs Personality Test? A test that results in four letters describing your personality type? You don't need to take it, I can tell you what your four letters are. They are the same as mine.

My score shows little ambivalence, and I am certain yours shows even less. Our personality type has a really strong sense of duty and loyalty. Most distinctly it expects a lot out of itself.

The one thing that always disturbed me about our four letters, through is that they don't encompass a big risk tolerance. It actually recommends occupations like accounting. It is a hard commitment to sustain, and you do it without giving yourself enough credit. And you are correct—I do things at LedgerPlus that I would NEVER do for/with anyone else. But I do them by myself for my practice, and I do them with much more enthusiasm with you since we can commiserate.

With respect to the funeral. It's really stressful to imagine you being under observation, and representing your country, and exhausted from travel, at the moment you were burying your close friend. And the specter of the General, your father-in-law, always there. I can honestly say that I can't imagine how tired and used up you felt. But I would bet that you didn't have much, if any, time to yourself to get a grip on it.

40

From: Robert H. Waldruff
Date: July 24, 2008
To: Paden Waldruff

Paden,

That night, I drank a few beers with a Basic School classmate who had flown in from Camp Lejeune for the funeral, Ed Waskiewiks. Ed had an MBA from Syracuse, and was actually recycled at OCS. UGH. Ed was a good guy. He was raised in an apartment in Utica, NY, located above his father's bar, Eddie's Place.

The next morning I had breakfast with Bob's brothers who didn't seem that emotional about things. The younger brother said he was going to join the Marines, but he never did. I never got to say goodbye to Bob's mother or father—too devastated. Shirley told me years later that Bob's father never got over this loss, but his mother finally got better after (she told Shirley) seeing Bob at the foot of her bed one night. He told her not to worry, that he was not in any pain and that he loved her. The mind is an amazing thing.

Shirley stayed in touch for several years. She even came to Camp

Lejeune for Christmas to see Mom and me, as it was three weeks before I was to go in for hopefully my final surgery. She would call periodically— the last time was when we lived in Richmond. I visited her in Arlington in 1988, when I was on a PW assignment in Dallas. She had married one of Bob's friends a couple years after his death; he was not like Woody, and our meeting wasn't that enjoyable. I wanted to talk about Bob, Shirley and Lisa. She felt awkward with this because of her husband, and we parted, both realizing time had moved on and we would probably never see each other again.

Bob's death and the escort and funeral was a huge deal in my life from several perspectives, not the least being an up close and personal experience of what the families go through when they have lost a child in war. Maybe now you understand a little better why touching Bob's name on the "black wall of death" was so emotional for me. It's a lot more than the loss of a good friend.

I was driven to the airport—can't remember by whom—and boarded a plane for LA to see you and Mom. Now I don't want to be overly dramatic. But here I was, having just buried my good friend. And knowing I was now going to Vietnam, not Okinawa like the first time (a place where people do get killed). And I was on my way to see my wife and never-before-seen child, and my mother and father. I would soon be saying goodbye to each of them for the second time, but now with the specter of fear a little more relevant. I mean, when I left the first time, it was off on this great adventure. Now it was "I need to get this over and get home to my family." The adventure had turned into an obligation, and a job to accomplish and get home.

I arrived at LAX and you were all there. I kissed Mom and carried you while talking about everything and nothing at the same time. Grandma and Grandpa took a backseat and let us do what we wanted. After a few days in L.A., you, Mom and I went to the folk's cottage at Lake Arrowhead for a few days alone, and they joined us for what was Memorial Day weekend. John and Sandy also came up. The two-plus days with you and Mom was bittersweet. It was great to be together, but all while knowing there was another separation looming.

We left Arrowhead on the day after Memorial Day and drove to Edwards AFB, near San Bernardino. We actually had to stop for a motorcade of Nixon and Thieu who had been in top-secret meetings over the weekend regarding Vietnam. I was dropped off at Edwards, and was to wait in my room until I could get a stand-by seat on a passenger plane to Okinawa. The goodbye was short and sweet. I've never liked goodbyes and this one needed to be over fast—too much emotion otherwise. A kiss goodbye, and a wave as you all drove off.

I had to wait two days for a flight and it was the loneliest time of my life. The loves of my life were ninety miles away and I couldn't be with them. I was tired out. The Wood affair kept playing in my mind, and I was headed for combat. I could only sleep a couple hours at a time and watch a little TV. I was very edgy wanting to get on with things. I couldn't indulge myself with thoughts of you and Mom, as duty was calling. I finally boarded my plane, and headed over to the Pacific for a second time in seven months. When we stopped in Hawaii to refuel, I hit the airport cocktail lounge and virtually chugged two double martinis. I got back on the plane, slept for a few hours, and endured.

We finally landed at Kadena AFB. I was taxied to the embarkation barracks for Marine officers leaving for Vietnam.

41

From: Paden Waldruff

Date: August 4, 2008

To: Robert H. Waldruff

Dear Dad:

Jesus Christ.

I feel like I could type for pages, but what would it amount to other than a wordy substitute for my semi-expletive above?

Edwards AFB—now I get why you asked me about it on Tuesday. I am anxious to check it out next time I am in the desert. How very strange that life has led me to the San Bernardino area, completely independent of your history.

So ... Kadena AFB ...

42

From: Robert H. Waldruff
Date: August 7, 2008
To: Paden Waldruff

Paden,

I spent the next day getting my shots, jungle utilities and boots, and my paperwork in order. That night at the staging barracks I had a few pops in the bar with a Major, Captain, and a couple of 1st Lieutenants, all of them slated to fly out the next morning. One of the Lieutenants was a basic-school classmate, and we caught up on names we both knew. This facility was weird. It was like a Hollywood movie. It was all screened in, tucked away under some trees. It was raining, and was very hot and humid. We called it a night early, and went to our rooms with our thoughts.

The next morning we got dressed and got driven to our flight. We boarded, buckled up, and headed for the Republic of South Vietnam. It was a Pan Am passenger plane complete with stewardesses and snacks. The flight wasn't long, only a couple hours I think. As we approached the coast of South Vietnam and the Da Nang airport, the pilot announced we would be landing soon. I looked out the window not knowing if I was looking at VC, NVA, South Vietnamese and/or all the above.

The country looked beautiful. The water was a gorgeous blue-green, and the countryside was covered with lush green vegetation. We began our descent, hit the ground, and taxied to the terminal. We deplaned, waited for our bags, and got on a truck headed for the 1st Marine Division compound. The airport was surreal. Marines and Vietnamese walking around with guns, looking and acting as though everything was normal. I, of course, tried to blend in and look and act like I was cool. But I really didn't know what to expect or say, so I pretty much just shut up. I know they all could tell I was a FNG— a F***ing New Guy.

You must remember, I was full of excitement and expectation. Finally, after Quantico, Fort Sill, Okinawa, and Japan I was going to a combat zone, to see with my own eyes what countless others had seen, experienced, and talked about. I would now be tested to see if I could apply my training to the real thing. And I'd test myself mentally and physically. The thought of getting wounded never entered my mind. All I really thought about was—when would the "action" start?

Before I forget. After this story is over, something that might be interesting for all of us would be for you to ask Mom her recollections of and feelings about these events. Now that I have shared with you, see if you can get her perspective.

I arrived at 1st Marine Division Headquarters, reported to

the Adjutant, got assigned a barrack. These were actually large screened huts with about twelve racks and lockers. I stowed my gear and set off to look up some guys I knew were here. I awaited an assignment to an artillery battery located in the field.

I caught up with Jeff Schmitt and Ed Zeigler. We talked of Woods' death and of what they knew about what was going on with the Corps in and around Da Nang. Ed was stationed with a motor transport unit at this base. Jeff was like me, in limbo waiting for orders to the field. I was here for about three or four days, during which we trucked off to see other Basic School classmates stationed in and around the base. We went shopping at Freedom Hill, the largest PX in the Marine Corps. That's where I bought the lamps we have in our bedroom. We went to movies at night, ate hamburgers, and drank beer at the Officers Club.

I was instructed that if the base got hit by mortars and/or sappers the alarm would sound, and I was to leave the barracks and get in the sandbagged area outside the front door. Jeff and I flew in a Huey gunship with the pilot whose mission was to fly to the rocket belt. This was an area where VC could hide their mortars within range of the base. His job was to fire his rockets and machine guns into suspected hideaways.

It was at this time I met Pete Grey over lunch at the mess hall. Pete had been president of the college at UVA— a big politico on Grounds. He was St A, Z Society, etc ..., and had gone to St. Christopher's School in Richmond where his father was a well connected attorney. He was in Force Recon. Their dangerous mission was to be inserted behind enemy lines and sneak around and gather intelligence on enemy activity. He was a great guy. He said he was torn between law school or an MBA, and seemed really interested in the University of Chicago. We wrapped up, said goodbye, and wished each other good luck. More about Pete later.

I finally got my assignment to a battery located on Hill 65. Marine batteries were always stationed in a static location, usually on a hill. The hills were named for their elevation above sea level. Hill 65 had a long history as it was close to An Hoa and the Arizona Territory. An Hoa was a Marine base regimental headquarters located right in the middle of an area that throughout the war was full of bad guys. The area was never really controlled by the Marines or by the VC. Many, many battles, both large and small, were waged there. Hence the name Arizona Territory—full of Indians. Its lore was profound throughout the Corps. Even today when I tell another Marine I was wounded in "The Zona", I get a knowing nod.

Morning arrived, and I was on a Huey off to An Hoa to check in, get my equipment, pistol and rifle and ammo and head for Hill 65. I felt like I was getting closer to the real deal!

43

From: Paden Waldruff

Date: August 21, 2008

To: Robert H. Waldruff

Dear Dad:

As you know, I hang on every word of these emails. I want to stop interrupting you with my sentence by sentence questions, and just listen to your story. But I need to come back for those answers when we are done.

Dad, I am so grateful that you are here to tell me, and I am grateful that we both know how much we love each other. I am starting to think that our project could be a pretty important contribution.

So, instead of trying to delay the inevitable (kind of joking, but part of me thinks I want to slow your story down with my questions so you don't get hurt), I will interject present tense moments that you can question (now or later).

Today.

This morning, I took the dogs for our walk at PVCC at around 8:30. I expected to be the only one there, as it was the weekend, but the theater parking lot was packed. Of course, I let the dogs out anyway and they ran off. Instantly three soldiers (Army) appeared to be following me and they called out, "Ma'am." I turned and walked toward them. I was excited to see them, and interested to know why they were there. Sadly, I could tell they were not looking forward to interacting with one of the crazy locals. It makes me really sad that within my lifetime those who serve and protect have been forced to add PR agent to their job description.

They said, "We just thought you should know that a chopper is going to be coming over the horizon in three minutes and landing in the field where your dogs are. Of course, you are welcome to do what you wish, but we thought you should know your dogs might be scared." I said, "Homecoming? Did you all just return from Iraq?" And it broke my heart when I saw them stiffen as they said, "Yes." I replied, "Thank you, and welcome home," and I shook their hands. They instantly relaxed and said, "It is good to be back.", and the chopper appeared. I screamed for the dogs to get the hell out of the way of important business, and the soldiers walked towards the field to receive the chopper.

So the dogs and I made it to the parking lot where the wives were gathering with their babies to watch. I got sucked into what was happening. It took several attempts to get the proper landing position before the three soldiers could approach. I was listening to a mother describe to her daughter that there was a General on the helicopter, and that he was coming to welcome her daddy home.

She was squatting down holding her toddler and I was squatting down holding the dogs' collars so they didn't bother anyone.

She and I caught each other's eye. She had tears streaming down her face, and for some reason I was already tearing up from listening to her. She said, "No one understands why I cry at the good moments. We all hear so much bad news. And I worry every day. I am used to it; I served too. I don't cry anymore from the bad news. I cry from the good news ... and no one knows or hears about that." I said, "I think I might understand what you are saying, and I am so happy that your husband and your daughter's father is home." And then I really made sure that the dogs and I were long gone before the General reached the theater.

Maybe I am also looping back to saying, I do want Mom's perspective.

Then I had another experience on that same day at a wedding that I want to tell you about, but I'll save it for next time.

Okay, so I just re-re-read your email and my fingers started typing, "You arrived on a commercial flight? Surreal." Then my mind was off to the races with a million other questions. But I am sticking to the plan.

44

From: Robert H. Waldruff
Date: August 25, 2008
To: Paden Waldruff

Paden,

When the Marines waded ashore on China Beach, there were hundreds of South Vietnamese civilians. For the record, I arrived "in country" on June 6, 1970. The Marines had been at Da Nang since the beginning of their involvement in Vietnam, March 1965. They landed an amphibious assault-force like in WWII. A lot was made of this attempt by LBJ to impress the NVA, as when he was on the beach giving leis to the Marines, making them look awkward and stupid. The Marine base at Da Nang had been there at least five years before I arrived, and was established and well-fortified. It was located in Quang Nam Province and, like I said, this entire province was heavily infiltrated with VC and NVA throughout the entire war. Of course this is where the Marines were sent, with the mission always being to locate, close with, and destroy. The area was heavily booby-trapped and a lot of Marines were killed or wounded by these traps. The enemy had many hiding places, both underground and in the mountains.

Like all the countryside in Vietnam, the terrain was inhospitable, with a lot of rice paddies, elephant grass, hedgerows, small villages, and rugged mountains. Whenever an operation was launched by Marines it was always rough going. By the time I arrived, the VC and NVA were hiding out and licking their wounds from heavy casualties suffered during the Tet offensive of February 1968. This is one of the tragedies of Vietnam. The US actually achieved a huge military victory during Tet, inflicting heavy losses on the NVA and almost wiping out the VC in many areas. The North had to start recruiting women and children to fill their ranks. However, the liberals and media told America it was a huge loss for the US. Walter Cronkite made his now-famous statement that we could not win and were locked in a stalemate.

Anyway, the VC and NVA were resting and regrouping for the continuation of their generational struggle, and were devoted to rebuilding their manpower and supplies of food and medicine.

My chopper flight from Da Nang to An Hoa took me over a lot of the "Arizona" and these "battlefields." It was an unbelievable sight, as the ground was covered with huge craters created by bombs and artillery shells. It looked like a moonscape. I wondered about the battles that must have occurred there. I landed on the airstrip in An Hoa and reported to the Executive Officer of the artillery battalion. Interestingly, I can't remember what battalion or battery I was assigned. I could probably figure out if I had to; I think it was Delta Battery, 2nd Battalion. The Major briefed me on activity in our TAOR (Tactical Area of Responsibility), primarily the An Hoa Basin and Que Son Mountains at one end, and Da Nang and the South China Sea at the other end.

My battery was located on Hill 65, where I would be choppered in the morning. Next stop was the supply tent where I got my pack, compass, e-tool (entrenching tool; a small shovel carried on the back with the pack), web belt, Ka-Bar knife, and other gear. Also, got my pistol; all Marine Officers carried a .45 caliber pistol with either shoulder holster or standard hip holster.

I went on a brief tour of the compound consisting of a lot of sandbagged fighting holes and tents. An Hoa was often attacked and mortared by the enemy, and was occasionally overrun, requiring hand-to-hand fighting. I got my rack assignment, and went to the mess tent for chow. There I talked to Marines who had been in-country for a while. They were matter of fact, no emotion, resigned to what was a boring and dangerous job. I grabbed a beer with the Major, and hit the rack wondering if I would ever see any bad guys or spend my remaining six months on Hill 65 working in the Battery (not to worry, as it turns out).

Next morning I got on a chopper to Hill 65. This base was smaller than An Hoa and not as fortified, but was heavily protected by concertina wire on the perimeter and fighting holes. As I flew in I could see six 105 howitzers, a lot of hooches, tents, several observation towers, and Marines walking around. Also stationed on this hill were the four infantry companies of 3rd Battalion, Fifth Marine Regiment, the mission security for the base. One company, I (India) was stationed on Hill 52 about five kilometers to the West (an outpost located on the Vu Gia river at the entrance to the Thuong Duc corridor) to protect against an enemy assault through Hill 52 on to Hill 55. As you see, I was going deeper into the labyrinth of danger, Da Nang, An Hoa, Hill 55 and eventually Hill 52.

I hopped off the chopper and checked in with the Battery CO, a Captain (I forget his name, too). The Captain gave me a quick briefing, saying he had all the officers he needed to man the Battery. I would instead be going to Hill 52 as the Forward Observer (FO) for India Company, 3rd Battalion, 5th Marine Regiment (I/3/5). It would probably be a couple of days before I'd leave. So I went to Officers hooch, grabbed an empty rack, stowed my gear, and started nosing around.

45

From: Paden Waldruff

Date: September 3, 2008

To: Robert H. Waldruff

Dear Dad:

Our project is always somewhere on my mind. The last time I wrote I was talking about the Army General landing at PVCC (weeks after the President's sleek, black helicopter flew over my house for the July 4, induction of new US citizens) to welcome home his troops.

The second part of what I wanted to share about that day was that I went to a wedding that evening. The bride is my friend so I spent most of my time meeting her family. Her sister served in the Air Force and is married to a man who just made Air Force Colonel. He also recently returned from Iraq, and their family just moved back to the US from England. You can imagine this resume was not what I expected to find in Charlottesville.

The Colonel was tasked with taking pictures of the event, and he seemed pretty happy to have a job as he floated through all of the people he didn't know with a beer in his hand. I talked to him for a few minutes; he was pretty worried about Russia. He was a good man.

Then I talked to one of the Aunts. She was quite extroverted—tough for me to handle—but at least she did most of the talking. She told me she lives in North Carolina, and I told her I was born there. After she sussed out where in North Carolina I was born and why, she was off to the races. She told me her husband had served in Vietnam. I think he is about five years older than you. He had never shared a single detail with her of what happened there. He was in the Coast Guard in Hawaii before Vietnam.

And then, much to my chagrin, she called her husband over for a conversation on the topic. He did what I could tell he has been doing to her for years, he blew her off on the topic.

Very inappropriate of the wife to put him in that position, I thought to myself. But it also got me thinking about some of the experiences you've had when you've mentioned your time to other men who served. And by that I mean, I most certainly did not mention the Arizona Territory.

When I was leaving, the aunt whispered in my ear, "Talk to your father."

When we started this project, I remember you telling me that there are so many books already on the subject. True, but not like this. And maybe we'll decide that we don't want the world to see our emails, or maybe we won't.

46

From: Robert H. Waldruff
Date: September 4, 2008
To: Paden Waldruff

Paden,

Everyone who went to Vietnam shares an experience, yet has a unique story. What you choose to do with our discourse is up to you. It is obviously very personal to me, and I've never shared such detail with anyone except Mom. Not even Mom has heard all I'm sharing with you. Not because I purposely have not told her. Maybe she thinks it's too personal; maybe she just wanted to move on and didn't see any value in going over history. The rehab period was emotionally traumatic for all of us, and I think we tried to put as much of the bad news behind as we could, and look forward to a bright and happy future.

I think in my heart of hearts I'll always be saddened by not having people treat us (me) as a hero. Not that I was anywhere close to a hero, but I felt I had done a good job when, in my opinion, a lot of my contemporaries were shirking their responsibilities. I mean, as recently as last month my barber asked where I got the scar in my scalp and ear. He thought maybe I'd fallen off a bike as a child. When I told him Vietnam, I wanted him to say, "Wow, you were there! Thanks! Our country never really appreciated what you guys did, etc ..." Instead he apologized for mentioning it, said it must really have been horrible over there, and then he changed the subject.

I think that's what Americans did to the Vietnam Vets. They changed the subject because of their guilt, and consequently shut the Vets out. "I don't want to hear about it!" So, the Vets don't talk about it; it's kept inside with obviously a lot of emotion. I tear up often when I read a poignant article or story about the Vietnam experience. Most Vets are not ashamed of our experience. Quite the opposite. We're quite proud of what we did.

The Left, with the My Lai story and pictures of civilians being killed and hooches torched, influenced a lot of people to think that Vietnam was an American mistake and we conducted ourselves shamefully. This was the narrative of a lot of those who didn't serve. Don't get me wrong. I didn't expect and/or want everyone slobbering all over me; just recognition. That's enough of that. I digress.

I'm intrigued and surprised you find this story so interesting. It gives me great joy to share it with you.

I walked around the compound, which consisted of a screened hooch mess hall, and several screened hooches where the Marines lived. There was a watchtower, with an integrated observation device, similar to the tower Bob Wood was in when he died. The infantry would stand guard in sandbagged fighting holes dug about three feet deep all around the perimeter 24/7. The infantry would also send out small squad-sized patrols every night to snoop around and deter the VC from infiltrating the compound.

I ran into a couple of Basic School classmates who shared their experiences since we departed Quantico, I to Fort Sill, they to Vietnam. I visited the Fire Direction Center (FDC). That was where the battery received "fire missions" from FOs. They plotted the map coordinates, then adjusted the artillery guns to fire rounds where the FO called for them.

There wasn't anything going on, as there were no Marine units out on an operation. Thus no contact was being made with the enemy, and no shooting was taking place. Things were very static with the enemy happy that the Marines were not on the offensive. I spent most of the next couple of days at the artillery hooch talking to the artillery lieutenants living there.

After a few days, the artillery CO called me into his "office" to inform me that the next day I would be assigned as the Forward Observer for India Company, 3d Battalion, 5th Marine Regiment stationed on Hill 52, about five kilometers from Hill 65. He briefed me that there was a lot of VC activity around Hill 52 and that it was the farthest west Marine outpost in Vietnam from which one could see Laos. Didn't know how long I would be there and/or what was next.

I was informed of the current "rules of engagement." They required approval from the Vietnamese before any artillery rounds could be fired, unless I/ my company was under attack. This was another ridiculous rule. I mean if I/my company commander suspected enemy activity, but we were not under attack, before I could fire artillery rounds on this suspected enemy position, my request had to be given to the chief of the closest village for his permission. Now not only did this process take time, sometimes hours, but it also alerted everybody around what was coming. If there was enemy activity, this process would allow them to be long gone before any artillery was fired. And, most village chiefs were Viet Cong; you can see why we couldn't win.

I left An Hoa the next morning on a Huey gunship helicopter headed for Hill 52. The ride was only about twenty minutes over rice paddies, past a few small villages, and up the Song Vu Gia river which had several boats fishing and trafficking in all directions. I would later find out a lot of these "fishermen" were Viet Cong gathering food for themselves and/or spying on US troop movements and operations. As I'm sure you've heard, a challenge of Vietnam was identifying friends from foe. The saying was, "farmers by day, Viet Cong by night."

I landed in my new home on about June 12, 1970.

47

From: Paden Waldruff

Date: September 4, 2008

To: Robert H. Waldruff

Dear Dad:

Oh, God. I am going first to your orders as you were deployed to Hill 52, and my mind is swirling after what I've just read. In internet shorthand, I would say "WTF" (what the F***?).

Based on the "rules of engagement" you described vs. reality, 1. In combat there is no time to check in for approval before firing, and 2. The check-in point is probably dirty. I have two troubling words in my mind for the entire India company: "sitting ducks." Therefore, I would naturally assume that "the rules of engagement" were frequently not observed.

I have thought a lot about the fact that politicians set the program, and the military enforces it. And while I know the military is consulted, it is ultimately the administration's call. Clearly, in my mind at least, the Vietnam War was the breaking-point for the alliance between the military and the politicians. Yes, I am calling out the weak liberals, and George Bush faced an impossible PR task. A tragedy on countless levels.

Dirtbags like Michael Moore produce crappy "documentaries" and say the US exploits our blue-collar folk. My question is, "Hey moron, who do you think was responsible for this transition? Who do you think destroyed patriotism?"

It breaks my heart on a number of different levels, as I know it does yours, to know that to this day your barber would prefer to change the subject.

But I am proud, and I have always been proud, of your honesty and boldness.

So, June 12, 1970 ...

48

From: Robert H. Waldruff
Date: September 8, 2008
To: Paden Waldruff

Paden,

I don't think patriotism has been destroyed. Rather, those hate-America liberals who were never patriots now think they are legitimized and politically correct because of the way Vietnam ended (the biggest champion being Slick Willie). They think they have the higher ground when criticizing US foreign policy vis-a-vis Iraq. I, for the life of me, will never understand how men of my generation not only avoided the draft, but protested against us. They thus aided the enemy and caused increased US casualties. How do they sleep?

Funny, when I was going through my process of signing-up for duty, I remember telling people I didn't want to be fifty years old when my children asked "Daddy, what did you do in the war?" and have to respond, "Nothing." Now you have asked.

The rules of engagement constraints were another huge criticism of LBJ as he literally day-by-day micromanaged the war. He had a map room in the White House, and got daily briefings. He gave the Joint Chiefs combat operation orders. He thought by "controlling" artillery fire, we would limit civilian casualties and increase our ability to win their hearts and minds. This was foolish, and despised by the military. General Fegan, although not being specific, would indicate that the USMC was concerned with the management of the war.

The Company Commander, Capt. Walker, met me at the helicopter landing zone. He introduced himself and gave me a situation report (sitrep) as we walked up the hill to the command bunker. Hill 52 was about the size of half a football field, and was 52 meters high at its apex. Funny you mentioned we were sitting ducks. The thought never entered my mind while on the Hill, and I never felt endangered. In retrospect, it was a very dangerous location.

As an aside, I was on this Hill for thirty days, and it was decided in about 90-120 days that the Army would relieve the Marines and take over responsibility for the outpost. As the Marines were pulling out of areas, the Army would move in and take over. I met the Army General who would be in charge of operations in this area, Lt. General Sutherland, as he visited the Hill and toured around and asked some questions. I read in the *Stars & Stripes* several months later that Hill 52 was overrun by the Viet Cong and seven soldiers were killed and several wounded. I think a big reason this didn't happen to the Marines was because of our tactics, diligence, and fire-power located on this Hill. It wasn't that the Army wasn't diligent, but that they just approached things differently.

On this hill was a Marine rifle company of three platoons, two 155 howitzers (bigger guns than the 105s back on Hill 65). We also had six ontos (vehicles similar to the Gator at the farm) that had four 106m recoilless rifles mounted on top. We were within fifteen minutes of a Phantom jet Air Force base, and of course had an artillery battery in support on Hill 65. The perimeter was heavily fortified with concertina wire, and Marines lived in bunkers on all sides of the Hill. Also, every night, squad-sized patrols were sent out to keep tabs on any possible infiltration, and daily patrols were sent into the hillsides next to us.

The Song Vu Gia trekked a straight path from Hill 65 to Hill 52 then turned right and passed directly in front before turning left and flowing down the Thuong Duc corridor. On the right were foothills sloping steeply upwards. In front and across the river was a flat land with a couple of small villages and rice paddies. On the left were the mountains with a huge ridge about half way up. The foothills on the right were the infamous "Charlie's Ridge" so named because the VC mostly controlled this rugged terrain throughout the war. FYI, the Viet Cong in military speak were "Victor Charlie" thus the various names of Charles, Charlie, Chuck, VC, etc …

The command bunker had a tarp on top and netting on the

sides for ventilation. The mosquitoes in Vietnam were ferocious and this netting protected us. Living in this bunker was the CO, me, Gunnery Sergeant, First Sergeant, and a couple of Corporal clerks. Underneath was another bunker with my radio operator and radio operations for the infantry. My operator was a borderline shitbird. It seems that in this bunker, pot was frequently used.

An interesting aside, this Marine was a card-carrying member of the Blackstone Rangers, a ruthless and powerful gang whose turf was the Blackstone area just south of the University of Chicago's campus. It seems two years ago while I was studying in the Business School library a couple blocks away, my radio operator was engaged in mayhem, drugs, murder, and destruction. I'm sure he was one to whom the judge said five to ten years, or enlist in the USMC.

Captain Walker was a good guy, nearing the end of his thirteen-month-tour. We were the types nobody wanted to be around, a new guy and a short-timer. For obvious reasons, we were vulnerable as the new guy didn't know anything and the short-timer tended to be overly cautious. One of the platoon commanders was a 2nd Lieutenant who graduated from UVA, a good guy who took care of his men.

The CO told me that the village off to the side of our hill had been the site of an enemy ambush on a Marine patrol and the FO had to call in artillery at night during the fight. I started studying my map, plotting coordinates of likely attack spots. The two 155s were manned by two artillery 1st Lieutenants from southern

California. It was quite unusual to have two guns away from a battery and stationed on a remote hill. They were there, I guess, in case we needed immediate support and/or were overrun. These guys were typical laid-back Californians, and because they were artillery types, I spent a lot of time with them in their bunker.

Down the river corridor was the Army Special Forces outpost of Thuong Duc. This was the same Thoung Duc where Marine Capt. Chuck Robb (later elected Governor of Virginia and US Senator) was assigned, however, that was earlier. The Army Special Forces were some tough dudes that were always stationed at dangerous, remote outposts. Thuong Duc was no exception as it was in the middle of a major VC sanctuary. Many nights we could see battles occurring by observing the tracer rounds of gunfire. Up on Charlie Ridge, easily seen from our Hill, was a cave where every now and then at night, the VC would roll out a recoilless rifle and fire down on Thuong Duc. We decided to see if we could take them out, and set the coordinates of their location on one of our 155s. After several nights they finally appeared and we fired five rounds. We never saw them again. I don't know if we took them out, but I guess we got their attention.

I asked the Captain if I could go on one of the night patrols. He said definitely not as I was more valuable as his FO. I fired some artillery into the heavily foliaged hillside on our right as this was a free fire zone. There were no Vils there, and thus we didn't need permission. These were coordinated with Marine patrols, and were fired into suspected enemy positions.

We got mail delivered every couple of days by helicopter during resupply missions. We ate basically C-rations, and some canned goods sent in from Hill 65.

One night a firefight broke out about five clicks to our side, across the river behind us and in the Arizona. We saw a lot of tracers; a Marine patrol had happened upon something. After a little while this huge plane appeared, and was firing tracer rounds as it lazily circled and floated around the area of contact. Seems this plane was a C-130 mounted with fifty-caliber machine guns. They were often used in Vietnam, and had the nickname "Puff the Magic Dragon" as they spit fire—a pretty awesome sight.

By the way, if you haven't already noticed, I am just relating memories as they come to mind, and in no special sequence.

I mentioned earlier that there was always activity on the river, mostly sampans and canoes. Some were probably legitimate fishermen, and some were VC, reconnoitering our Hill and commandeering food supplies from the peasants. One day we saw very suspicious activity of what sure looked like VC massing boats across the river. We got suspicious, and the CO called for a phantom air strike primarily to scatter the boats and let them know we were watching. About fifteen minutes later, two Phantom jets appeared over our position. We were all sitting on top of the bunkers to witness the show. They did a snake and nape (snake-eye rockets and napalm) on the area. They were so close that shrapnel flew onto our hill. What a show of power! Needless to say, all VC activity stopped. When they finished they flew right over our Hill at about fifty feet off the ground, tipping their wings as they roared past. I'll never forget it; it seemed we could almost touch their wings.

Another day we saw smoke down the Thuong Duc corridor out towards Laos. We felt the ground rumble, and finally, the faint noise. This was a B-52 bombing attack, called an Arc Light. They were pretty common during the war. I often thought that if the ground was shaking five miles away, what was it like for any VC located within the target area? Truth was, it took so long to get approval—five hours—that most of these strikes were known long before they occurred, and so the VC had already scrammed. Still, even if they were underground in tunnels, their brains must have gotten a little scrambled! The awesome fire power of the battlefield.

After two weeks, I got to fly back to Hill 65 for a shower and some hot chow and check in with the battery CO. I'll never forget the feeling I had as I hopped off the helicopter with my dark tan. My pistol was strapped to my waist, a couple weeks in "the bush" and walking towards the battery, "like a rock ... eighteen, lean and solid everywhere." I felt invincible and salty, really finally feeling like a combat Marine. However, I still had not been in a fight, and still had not had to call in artillery in an attack situation.

Patience, young man; be careful what you wish for!

49

From: Paden Waldruff

Date: September 15, 2008

To: Robert H. Waldruff

Dear Dad:

Oh wow; I totally identify with the last passage!!!

And what a nerve-wracking scenario.

Was there significant down-time? If yes, what did you do, especially as the new guy?

What was it like trying to fall asleep at night?

50

From: Robert H. Waldruff
Date: September 24, 2008
To: Paden Waldruff

Paden,

Remember I told you the saying that war is 90 percent boredom and 10 percent utter terror? Well, for me, Hill 52 was boring. I suspect the grunts and the Company CO had a somewhat more interesting time, with taking care of their men, patrolling, and guarding the perimeter. I had almost nothing to do. My job as an artillery FO was to support infantry operations with artillery as the situation demanded. Well, there were no operations going on at Hill 52. This was a static position in place to protect against any enemy attacks, none of which occurred during my 30 days on the Hill.

By the way, the Hill also had an Army of Vietnam (ARVN) artillery battery of six 105 howitzers. My day was occupied with reading pocket-books and magazines, writing letters, reading letters, roaming around talking to the other Marines on the Hill. It was ungodly hot and sleeping was no problem as I had a cot in the bunker and at night a breeze picked up, and the netting kept the mosquitoes at bay. The Captain would get up during the night to check with his platoon commanders via radio, and would patrol the perimeter to be sure everybody was awake and in position. I remember thinking that I had probably missed all the action, but at least I got to Vietnam.

One night, Captain got word there was suspicious noise and movement off the front of the hill. We went over to the spot, talked to the platoon commander, and listened. Captain got the Marines closest to the noise to lock and load and get ready to fire. He also moved the ontos into position and aimed their guns down the hill towards the activity. I was preparing to call in artillery if indeed we were attacked. Captain was cautious, fearing they might be Marines. We kept trying to make radio contact with the patrol that had left earlier. Just before we were about to open fire, the squad leader of the patrol made radio contact. It seems he had gotten disoriented and turned around, and was coming towards the Hill instead of away! We laughed later but it could have been a disaster.

Mail was very important. I kept all my letters and read them many times. I got most from Mom, but Grandma and Grandpa wrote, and aunts and uncles wrote. I don't remember college friends writing. I corresponded with the University of Chicago about using their Job Placement Program when I got discharged. Of course, Larry and Sandy wrote, too.

Every morning would begin with men carrying mine sweepers

cleaning up the road from Hill 55 to Hill 52. The road was used mostly by locals. We celebrated the Fourth of July with cases of warm beer, dehydrated steaks, and shrimp. It was a meal fit for kings. There were "pet" dogs on the Hill to occupy our attention. I've got several photos of life on Hill 52, if you're ever interested. One Corporal lost a leg on a patrol in the mountains next to us as he hit a mine, and had to be medivac-ed out. Kind of rough.

I guess today I'd be spending time on my cell phone. I was, however, gaining wisdom and knowledge of what being a Marine in Vietnam was about, by talking and listening to the Captain and other officers on the Hill. This boredom is why the Phantom jets attack was so exciting—it was something different. Around the 8th of July we were informed that India Company was being replaced on the Hill by K(Kilo) Company, 3rd Battalion, 5th Marine Regiment. India Company would return to Hill 65.

Word was that India Company would be conducting an operation in the Arizona. It would be the first company-sized operation in the An Hoa Basin in almost six months. Now, this would be some exciting news, if true. It meant that I would be an FO accompanying them—a Marine infantry company in the notorious "bad lands" of the Arizona. This was an opportunity either envied or pitied by the Marines of Hill 65.

Kilo arrived by foot on the road from Hill 65, and India departed. I remained on Hill 52 for an extra day to brief the new FO and particularly the new CO. The new CO was a senior

Captain just in country for his second tour. It seems he was wounded during his first tour. He was married with children; a nice guy, and serious. I've often wondered how I would have felt, after having been seriously wounded, leaving you, Tucker, and Mom for a second tour. I don't think I would have been gung-ho!

The next day I left by chopper for Hill 65, and hooked up with the new CO in the officers' hooch. This guy was a 1st Lieutenant with about twelve months on me. He had been in Vietnam for about eight months, and seemed to know his stuff. He confirmed we would be helo-lifted across the Vu Gia into the Arizona tomorrow morning. Our mission was to provide security for Vietnamese villagers from My Hiep, as they harvested a corn crop from a lush area that had been planted by the Viet Cong. This was to demoralize the VC as they desperately needed the corn crop and had been protecting it for several months anticipating its harvest. This was also to give confidence to the locals that they need not fear the VC, as the Marines would be their protectors.

I remember thinking this sure wouldn't be much, and almost laughing that we big bad Marines would be standing around like policemen. As I found out years later, this was actually a very important operation. And as I found out in a few days, it was a very dangerous one.

On my way to the battery, I ran into Dennis Mroczkowski. As with Bob Wood, we went through OCS, TBS, and Ft. Sill together. A good guy and good Marine. We caught up on classmates and some other info. I told him about my mission, and he told me he was leaving tomorrow to be an FO with an ARVN unit. We wished each other luck and shook hands. It was many years before I knew what happened to Dennis.

I spent some time with the battery commander and joined my infantry company officers for a night's sleep prior to our adventure.

51

From: Paden Waldruff
Date: October 5, 2008
To: Robert H Waldruff

Dear Dad:

Many thoughts, as usual, were drifting through my mind as I was reading. But they don't really seem worth bringing up at the moment as I couldn't help but zero in on the last part of the email.

Your assignment made the hairs rise on my neck. You've foreshadowed it a little bit, so I can understand how you initially perceived it. BUT, you were taking a crucial food source from the VC, and for lack of a better word, emasculating them. It was clearly a good tactical move, but still hair-raising.

I am picturing a wide open space with locals—locals who could have VC among them—harvesting in the center. The Marines guarding the perimeter, in the hot sun.

Dear God.

52

From: Robert H. Waldruff
Date: October 6, 2008
To: Paden Waldruff

Paden,

The following information has been acquired over the years, through books on the history of Vietnam. Almost none of it did I know at the time of our operation. First, a correction on my last installment. The Captain I talked about on Hill 52 was not my FO replacement, but was the Company Commander of Kilo Co. FOs were almost always 2nd Lieutenants or 1st Lieutenants and not Captains. As a matter of fact, my replacement on Hill 52 was a Sergeant—not even an officer.

Big Picture. From reading the book *A Better War*, I learned that after the fall of 1968, Army General Creighton Abrams relieved General Westmoreland and a sweeping tactical change occurred. Whereas Westmoreland favored large unit operations, Abrams believed in small-unit tactics. This was driven by the reality that the Viet Cong and NVA were not capable of large-unit operations post-Tet due to the massive losses they suffered.

Abrams' and the Marines' tactics in 1970 were small-unit operations to disrupt the supply lines of the enemy, and to work with the civilians to gain their trust. It was also important to work with the local militia as the US would be leaving a lot of the fighting to the South Vietnamese sooner rather than later due to the changing political climate in the US. This was called the "Vietnamization" of the war. Of course, the South was not ready, but reality was what it was. These small-unit tactics, combined with the weakened enemy due to Tet, were succeeding on an ever-increasing scale. We were starting to win the war. It's been argued that if we had employed an Iraqi-type surge, victory would have been at hand. That's another story.

The Smaller Picture. The 5th Marines battled the VC and NVA in the northern Arizona for most of 1969, particularly in the second half of 1969, in the same area I was soon invading. There were several company-sized operations with heavy casualties on both sides, but the Marines were coming out ahead. Starting in 1970, the skirmishes were on a smaller scale, with a lot of Marine actions consisting of flying low in Huey gunship helicopters and picking off enemies one by one. However, the northern Arizona remained infested with Viet Cong and NVA infiltrating from sanctuaries on Charlie's Ridge with trails leading down to the Arizona.

Around May 31, 1970, VC infiltrated the perimeter of An Hoa. It seems the Marines were onto this early on. They let the infiltration occur, luring the VC into a killing zone with several casualties ensuing. Around June 25-26, while I was on Hill 52, a small Marine unit went into the northern Arizona in search of weapon and food storage areas. They hooked up with another Marine unit to spoil a VC attack on Hill 55. I now think this was the activity we witnessed when Puff the Magic Dragon was called in. I also think the suspicious activity we saw on the Vu Gia when we called in the air strike was probably part of a coordinated effort to assault Hill 55. Obviously, the attack on Hill 55 was foiled.

Remember, at the time I knew none of this! So, unknown to me and probably all of India company, we were heading into an area with probably a 100 percent chance of enemy contact. The corn crop was vital to both the VC and NVA. Vital as in life or death. This was their neighborhood, and it would be fatal to them for our mission to succeed.

Our Picture. Our operation was named Barren Green. I did not know this until about five years ago. We were the tip of the spear for a larger operation called Pickens Forest, which was a battalion operation into NVA sanctuaries in the Que Son mountains. We were accompanied by RFs (local militia from the region called Regional Forces) and PFs (locals from the province called Provincial Forces). This was to boost their confidence, and to show the civilians that these forces could help protect them. These guys were a joke. They traveled with chickens and pigs, even some family members. They were probably mostly VC sympathizers. Nonetheless, they followed behind our column.

I picked up a new radio operator. It seems the battery commander knew my Hill 52 guy was a shitbird, and he asked for volunteers. Only one Marine spoke up. I can't remember his name, but he was a good young man. Seems his brother had been a Marine in Vietnam and had returned home with a medal. This young man wanted to live up to his brother's legacy.

As often happens, the official and actual timelines of our operation differ. Officially, the operation took place July 15—16, 1970. Actually, it took place July 15—18, 1970. My Purple Heart is dated July 15, but I'm sure it was July 17. If it truly was July 15, then the operation took place from July 13-16. Amazing.

Anyway, we awoke the morning of July 13 or 15, had breakfast, and headed down to the waiting choppers. A fully-armed combat-ready Marine rifle company in Vietnam was quite a sight. Everyone had an M-16 rifle, as many magazines as he could carry, machine gunners, 60mm mortars with rounds.

I also carried an M-16 to disguise myself as much as possible from enemy snipers, by looking like a grunt. Obviously, prime targets were the company commander and FO. Were pretty easy to identify as we walked together, and both of us had radio operators with long antennae sticking in the air. I had my pistol in my pocket; the pistol was another sure give-away of officer status. I also wore my Ka-Bar Marine knife. Of course I had a compass, binoculars, and a map.

We also had two Sergeants, who were FOs for 81 millimeter

mortars. These were much smaller firepower than 105 artillery howitzers, but they could fire rounds faster due to less adjusting of the guns. We all had flak jackets and metal helmets, and as many canteens of water as we could hump. We also carried several C-ration containers.

We boarded the choppers, about forty Marines per bird and about a hundred or so Marines in all. We would meet the PFs and RFs in the village. We lifted off over the Vu Gia into the northern Arizona on that hot July morning not knowing our fate. Nor did we know that a Viet Cong battalion and members of the so-called "elite" NVA 38th Regiment awaited our arrival.

53

From: Paden Waldruff
Date: October 6, 2008
To: Robert H. Waldruff

Dear Dad:

Once again, Jesus Christ.

And once again, I have a lot of questions, but we can come back to them later.

I've never experienced a firsthand account that included the author working to recall his memories as he was realizing what history says.

Forty Marines per bird makes a hundred plus Marines. Marines with a touch of an eye-roll at their police duty in a corn field, not knowing that they were representing a major tactical change in the strategy. Do you think that was a good thing or bad thing? Clearly this was an important, dangerous mission. When you mention the waiting VC and NVA, do you have any concept of numbers?

Enough questions that I said I wouldn't ask.

Please continue.

54

From: Paden Waldruff
Date: October 6, 2008
To: Robert H. Waldruff

Cringing, that I haven't memorized this, and I don't even know how to ask. Forgive me for not figuring out how to phrase this. What do you tell another Marine who asks what group you were with?

55

From: Robert H. Waldruff

Date: October 20, 2008

To: Paden Waldruff

Paden,

I thought you asking questions was a part of this dialog—a speaking for your generation kind of thing.

Marines identify their service by what regiment they were in. A regiment designation is unique, whereas each regiment has a 1st, 2nd, and 3rd battalion and each battalion has the same four (lettered) companies, e.g., 5th Regiment, 3rd Battalion had I, K, L and M companies and 7th Regiment, also has a 3rd Battalion that also has I, K, L and M companies. Each Marine Division has four infantry regiments and one artillery regiment.

The Marine regiments each have a unique service history of different battles and wars in which they served. The "Fighting Fifth" Marine Regiment is the most decorated regiment in Marine Corps history. As a result of saving the French from Germany in WW1, the French awarded the regiment the French fourragère, which is a short green braided rope worn by current members of the 5th Marines over their shoulder on their green uniforms. General Fegan was a company commander in the 5th Marines when wounded in Korea. Although I was in an artillery regiment, probably the 12th Marines, because I was an FO, I was assigned to Company I, 3rd Battalion, 5th Marine Regiment. Sooo, when I would talk to someone who knows what's going on, I would tell him I was with the 5th Marines in Vietnam.

Now on with the story.

Your question regarding what I thought of the "new" tactical strategy. My opinion is prejudiced by General Abrams' book wherein he makes a compelling argument for its success. My personal experience would argue it wasn't so successful! After a short flight from Hill 65 over the Vu Gia river, we landed in a clearing, saddled up, and began our hump to the corn fields of the My Hiep village.

A Marine company would hump by spreading out single-file, each Marine about six feet from the man in front. This was done because if a Marine would hit a mine the other Marines would be far enough away to not get hit. Also if the enemy should open up fire they couldn't kill two Marines with the same gun burst. Landmines in the Arizona were an omnipresent threat and a worrisome concern of all Marines. Each step was taken not knowing if it would land on a mine and/or trip over a wire which would detonate a mine.

You can imagine a hundred plus Marines spread out over 600

feet was a lot for the company commander to control. This task was done through communication and control with the three platoon commanders who were 2nd Lieutenants. We were humping through jungle and walking on a trail. That's usually not a good idea, as trails are easy to booby-trap, but it meant we didn't have to cut our way through the foliage.

The most challenging position in this type of operation was the Marine who walked point. Any booby trap, ambush, sniper attack, etc. was probably going to kill this individual. There are many stories about these types. Most relished the challenge, and, I guess, met it with a touch of fatality. It was a crucial responsibility that required a sixth sense as to whether the column was approaching danger or not. There was constant stopping while this Marine would check the trail and jungle out in his front. Everyone was also checking out the jungle on either side. An ambush could easily occur anywhere, because we could only see about six feet through the jungle. This formation was practiced many times during my basic school training, and although it was my first such operation in Vietnam, it was a very familiar situation. Except this wasn't training; it was for keeps.

As I mentioned, it was incredibly hot and humid and although everyone was aware of water conservation, we were emptying our canteens pretty fast. About a mile in, the point-man felt suspicious about some movement in front of him. The CO told me to call in some artillery at the head of the column. Now, the map I had was old and not totally accurate. Typical of most maps of Vietnam, it was made by the French, decades before. This was the first "real fire" shot I'd ever called in. A mistake in calling in the map coordinates could result in artillery rounds landing on our column and wounding Marines.

Due to the extensive training I had received at Fort Sill, Japan, and Okinawa, I felt pretty confident. I located the coordinates on the map that were in front of the column, and had my radio man call in the fire mission to the battery. After a few minutes the rounds whistled over our heads and landed exactly where the point-man wanted. I remember to this day my anticipation prior to the rounds landing. After the impact, I started to feel pretty confident that I definitely knew what I was doing. I also suspect the CO was relieved, as he had not known beforehand whether I knew my stuff or not. He was now starting to gain confidence in me also.

We continued to hump for about two or three hours, and hit a clearing surrounded by thick jungle. The CO ordered a halt to rest up for a while. Just as everyone started to sit down, automatic weapon fire opened up on us from the jungle to our front. We had not formed a perimeter, which I remember thinking was kind of basic tactics at Basic School. Maybe lots of times in Vietnam it wasn't done. Regardless, everyone started to scramble. The Marines closest began returning a heavy volume of fire, and the enemy fire ceased. This was probably an advance scout team of Viet Cong testing our readiness and fire-power. I don't think we felt this at the time; maybe we thought it was a couple of VC trying to harass us.

You asked if I knew how many VC and/or NVA awaited us. At the time, no. Based on subsequent information, I know it was at least one VC Battalion and "elements" of an NVA regiment. Even at full-strength, a VC battalion was a lot smaller than a Marine battalion. I never saw any information on how many elements of NVA were on the ground. If I had to guess, I would say a total of 50 to 70. Remember though, there were hundreds of reinforcements not far up their trail-network, under cover in the foothills of the mountains.

An aside, in 1969, the Marines created a ribbon called the Combat Action Ribbon. It was awarded to any Marine or sailor involved in hostile action with an enemy where fire was received and returned. It had to represent a legitimate threat on one's life. This ribbon was created to differentiate those Marines who served in Vietnam but never saw combat from those who served and actually saw combat. Well, after this episode and as we were saddling-up to continue our hump, my UVA 2nd Lieutenant friend went by and said he heard we all were going to qualify for the Combat Action Ribbon as a result of this enemy contact. We obviously weren't too worried about what just happened!

We continued our trek, and eventually went through the village of My Hiep, to the outskirts, and ended up at the edge of a huge corn field. It was mid-to-late afternoon, and the CO said we would set up a perimeter and stay here for the night. The location was in a clearing with the corn field surrounding about half of it, and dense jungle surrounding the other half. The three platoon commanders each took one-third of the perimeter, and spread their Marines out to guard us. The CO and I, our radio operators, and the company Gunnery Sergeant set up in the middle of the perimeter.

We were pretty much out of water, so we sent some Marines down through the jungle to the Vu Gia to fill up everybody's canteens. Now the Vu Gia, like all Vietnam rivers, was full of human and animal waste and sewerage. To "purify" this water for drinking, we put in a halazone tablet which dissolved and cleaned it up. I often wondered what could have been in those tablets! Anyway, we were so thirsty nobody really thought much about it.

After setting my pack down and getting out some C-rations I noticed everybody had their E-tools out, and they were digging sleeping holes for protection during the night if we were attacked and/or mortared. Acting like I did this all the time, I got my shovel and dug a long, narrow, deep hole to lie in. This took a considerable amount of time and energy. Anyway, everybody got dug in, ate their C-rations, and engaged in small talk. Daylight disappeared, and the sounds and darkness of the jungle engulfed India Company.

56

From: Paden Waldruff
Date: November 2, 2008
To: Robert H. Waldruff

Dear Dad:

This installment is chilling, I've read it many times.

I think the most amazing thing about what you've been writing to me over the past year is your ability to tell me about each step in this journey in the mindset you had as you were experiencing it.

I am sure you have gone over and over many of the details and experiences in your mind as the decades have passed. Yet your writing voice is clear, honest, without vanity, and present in each moment, even with the details you've recently learned from Abrams' book and all of the other influences of the past thirty-eight years.

I feel very fortunate, and know that I am the accountable person I am, because of who my parents are. I am so proud to be you and Mom's daughter.

On the other hand, our project is driving home that history is a personal narrative. I've made an effort to cast a wide net in my life of meeting and learning about people. My conclusion has never wavered that you are an exceptional individual. I feel so grateful that you are sharing this history with me.

Okay. I'm ready for you to proceed.

57

From: Robert H. Waldruff
Date: December 2, 2008
To: Paden Waldruff

Paden,

You won't believe this, but I just finished a very long chapter and during its composition I lost my internet connection. I continued on, not realizing that if I did not reconnect, my words would not be saved. Well, now I realize I've just wasted ninety minutes. No, I'm not pissed much. Plus, I'm not sure the second will be as good as the first! Anyway, here we go again.

Our first night was somewhat uneventful, even though we heard a couple of loud explosions. We surmised the VC were trying to launch a bomb from their mountain sanctuary, but couldn't get enough force behind it to reach our position. The night was hot, and as I lay in my hole I sprayed Marine-issue bug spray over all exposed skin. Thank God I did, as all night, swarms of mosquitoes circled my head buzzing loudly. But no bites.

I was feeling very little fear, still thinking this operation was not going to provide a lot of action. Not that I even knew what a lot of action was. Now, in retrospect, this is pretty interesting since we had already come under direct enemy fire. I, and everyone else I think, felt this was the result of a couple of VC local farmers and was meant as harassment and not much more. Also, remember I have learned a lot more about the danger of this area by reading some history.

By the way, I appreciate the feedback on my style of sticking to the facts without a lot of exaggeration. I've been fearful that I would get too emotional and/or dramatic.

We got out of our holes in the pre-dawn, ate some C-rats and coffee for breakfast, and got ready for the day. The CO met with his platoon commanders and went over the day's mission of providing security. Around 9 a.m. the local mayor arrived with a group of men and women civilians. They carried baskets with rope to attach them to their heads, and headed into the corn fields to begin harvesting the corn. Marines spread out behind these folks and focused on the jungle in the rear, which was very dense.

Before I forget, we all were wearing flak jackets weighing twenty pounds or more, making the mission even more fun.

The civilians started picking the VC's and NVA's vital and long-coveted corn crop. The CO sent a squad to patrol the other perimeter of the cornfield, about a mile away, to see if the VC would try to attack from that side. I spent time reviewing the map trying to orient it to the terrain. I wanted to be sure to correct any coordinate discrepancies, in the event I would have to call in some artillery.

A few uneventful hours passed. I remember talking to the Lieutenant, but can't recall what we talked about—I assume our families and home. Here we all were in a foreign land with plenty of bad guys all around us. The only thing in common was we were all Marines dedicated to ourselves and our mission and staying alive. Also, keep in mind ours was but a small operation in the six years Marines operated in northern South Vietnam. There were many larger and more important ops. But at the time, this one seemed real enough.

We received radio contact from the patrol. They had spotted some VC, and had received some fire. We could see them from our position, and I was pretty sure I knew where the VC were located. The CO said to go ahead and call in some rounds, which I had my radio man promptly do. It had been a few minutes, and we did not hear the guns. My radio-man said there was a Marine Major on the phone wanting to know who authorized this fire mission. Remember that I told you about the rules of engagement requiring being under enemy fire before an artillery mission could be authorized. I grabbed the phone, being quite pissed off. I told the Major that I was 1st Lieutenant Robert H. Waldruff, Service Number 0110047, and I was authorizing this fire mission.

I guess this worked, because soon rounds were fired, though they were a little short of the target. I adjusted the coordinates, and said fire for effect. Rounds landed right on target and the shooting stopped. I called in one more mission just in case. It was now obvious Victor Charles was all around us, and that he was quite pissed-off and dedicated to defeating our mission.

Late-afternoon sniper fire and automatic weapon fire opened up from the jungle to our right. It was aimed at the civilians, who dropped their baskets and ran towards us for protection. I'll never forget seeing a young attractive woman running through the corn and receiving a bullet wound right in the middle of her chest. It was very unusual to see an attractive peasant woman, as life was hard there and most were very rough-looking. We fired into the jungle, but couldn't see a thing because of the dense cover.

The firing stopped. A medic administered some first aid, and we called in a medivac chopper which flew the woman to the hospital. I have no idea if she made it. Needless to say, the civilians were not impressed with our security efforts. They left the fields, returning to their village of My Heip never to return. The rest of the afternoon, Marines picked corn.

I was no longer concerned about seeing real action. I was pre-occupied with the current situation, which was becoming increasingly dangerous. More VC and NVA moved toward our position, and they seemed more and more dedicated to seeing our mission fail. I had spent a lot of the day plotting coordinates on my map of likely enemy attack routes, in case I needed to call in a mission in a hurry. We decided to spend another night in the same perimeter, which was probably not wise as the enemy was gaining increasing knowledge of our troop strength, capabilities, and positions. The night passed uneventfully except for the mosquito swarms.

The next day, day three, included a visit from battalion headquarters consisting of the CO, who was a Lieutenant Colonel, and his staff of several majors and captains. Their chopper arrived late morning. Our CO met the Lt. Colonel and spent time briefing him of our situation and receiving instructions regarding our mission. I was somewhat detached as my chain of command went through the artillery battalion and the Colonel had nothing to talk to me about. I'm sure the major with whom I "chatted" on the radio the day before was eyeballing me. After a lot of talk and walking around, the Brass boarded their chopper and returned to safety.

As part of their mission, they took four or five bushels of freshly picked corn. We heard it was going to the Commanding General to eat with his evening meal. That was a good brown-nose for the Lt. Colonel. We also heard the whole staff was included in the Action Report, as they could document they were on the ground with India Company on July 15, 1970. They thus qualified for the Combat Action Ribbon. In retrospect, I think this visit and the official record showing Barron Green commenced on July 15, 1970, were somehow intertwined.

I've wondered if the contact we received the first two days was more than anyone predicted, and thus our mission became worthy of a name. Even though I've stated our mission was far from the largest and most important Marine operation, it was nonetheless an important mission with plenty of enemy contact. That involved us in something thousands of Vietnam Marines never saw, including my friend Bob Wood.

Our CO informed us that the Colonel had ordered us to hump a couple clicks deeper into the Arizona. We were to spend the night in a new location, fearing an enemy attack if we remained here much longer. We began to shut down this site. We filled in all our sleeping holes with dirt, and started organizing our gear for the hump. The battalion left us a Husky armored vehicle for our use—a tracked armor-plated vehicle with a seat in front and a scooped out storage area in the rear. Its primary benefit was a .50-caliber mounted machine gun, giving us significantly more firepower as we moved on. The party had also brought us large cans of assorted juices. This was pretty stupid. Whatever we couldn't immediately drink was left behind and buried, being too heavy to hump with all our other gear.

The time was around 2 p.m. on July 15, 1970.

58

From: Paden Waldruff

Date: December 15, 2008

To: Robert H. Waldruff

Dear Dad:

Thank you again for making the time to send me these emails. The word "priceless" doesn't even feel sufficient.

I love you so much and am so grateful that you and Mom are my parents.

I hope you and Mom are proud of me; if you are, you should really be proud of yourselves. Lord knows you were both forced to put a lot of work into the project. Thanks for sticking with me.

So, back to our project. I actually sat back and involuntarily clapped my hands as I was reading the following:

"I grabbed the phone being quite pissed-off and told the Major I was 1st Lieutenant Robert H. Waldruff, Service Number 0110047, and I was authorizing this fire mission." That is so you, and I am right there with you.

And, of course, my heart flinched as you were describing the woman who had a bullet rip through her—rough. And the image of the US flying a civilian out for medical care is not one that is commonly portrayed in our popular culture. Hmmm, I wonder why that is?

I love all of the details you are giving me.

59

From: Robert H. Waldruff
Date: December 19, 2008
To: Paden Waldruff

Paden,

Of course Mom and I are proud of you, and for many reasons. But, your personal values are yours and their consequences fall on you. Choose the moral path, and things will be okay.

There we were, arranging our packs and other gear just kind of milling around. We were waiting to move out, when the jungle to our side roared with automatic weapon fire. Everyone of us did the instinctive thing and hit the dirt. Now, since we had just covered our fighting holes, we had no protection. We were right in the open, like sitting ducks. We had been careless, and our enemy had carefully set this trap. It turns out it was a well-concealed and fortified VC Battalion and supporting elements of the well-trained and well-equipped North Vietnamese Army.

These soldiers had observed our behavior for two days, knew our strength, and had sprung this surprise attack with much planning. I was scared to death. Bullets were literally flying all around us from very short range. The sound was deafening, and gaining in intensity. Previously, the attacks had been short-lived and not really intense. This was different, as it was more weapons than before and not going away. They had us pinned down, and at a severe disadvantage. I remember digging at the earth and thinking this was serious. Something had to be done fast, or we were going to have a lot of casualties. We needed to get a lot of firepower on their position and fast.

Now there wasn't a whole lot of thought and planning going on. We were all reacting, and, without knowing at the time, using our instincts and Marine training. This was what my last two years of training had been all about. Of course every Marine was looking to the two officers for leadership and courage. The CO got his M-16 raised, got up, and yelled at the Marines close by to get up and lay down a blanket of fire. Then he charged right into the teeth of the enemy position. It was about the bravest thing I've ever witnessed.

At about the same time, I got up and ran to the two Corporals responsible for calling in 81mm mortar rounds. The 81mm mortars were much smaller than the 105mm artillery howitzers. They could be adjusted and prepared for firing much faster. Time was definitely of the essence, and I knew we had to get rounds on the VC fast. I made this decision without a lot of pondering. It was the right decision, and probably saved some Marine lives. Maybe mine also. To this day, I am very proud of this action.

At the time, I never thought about getting shot. But automatic weapon rounds were blanketing the clearing, and I'm sure I was a target by standing up and being the FO. If they get me, they knock out a lot of firepower. When I got to the two Corporals, they were terrified—frozen and eyes wide-open. I grabbed their radio headset and called in a fire mission. I had to take a quick look at the map, and called in the coordinates where I felt the VC were entrenched. There was no time to adjust fire, so these rounds had to be right on target.

In a very short period of time, rounds were fired and hit exactly where I wanted them. At the same time, I gave a fire mission to my radioman for artillery rounds. This kid was great; he got right up with me and followed me across the clearing, despite the gunfire. The battery was on their game; the rounds came out pretty fast, and again were right on the target. I called for several more missions. The VC fire started to slow down, and eventually stopped. This whole action might have taken ten minutes or more. Due to the CO's and my actions, no Marines were lost. I would only tell members of my family this seemingly bragging statement. I don't know how many enemy were killed, maybe none. They were notorious for dragging their dead away to deny us the satisfaction of knowing we had killed some of them.

We got back to our preparations to move out, but were a lot more cautious and on defense. There now was no doubt in any of our minds that we were being targeted by a very determined enemy cadre. I didn't think about this action the rest of the day, and not much for the next few weeks, being occupied with some other issues. It really came naturally and just seemed like a normal response under the circumstances. The next time I really felt proud of this, and that maybe it was a little out of the ordinary, was when General Fegan presented me with the Bronze Star Medal and read the citation referencing this action. Throughout my life I think of this attack and reflect on a couple of things.

Remember the leadership test at OCS that I told you about, the field problem. Four candidates with their backs turned were told to turn around. A name was shouted out, and that person was to take charge and solve an impossible problem. When I was called, I froze. This simulation was supposed to reveal what an individual would do in a combat situation when immediate action and leadership would be required. According to my OCS performance, I would come up lacking in a combat situation. However, I reacted calmly, intelligently and efficiently when it counted. I thus vindicated my poor performance on the field problem. I still think it was a stupid test, and I failed because I tried to overthink the solution. But, maybe that was the lesson: don't over think but react.

My other reflection was about passing the ultimate Marine test, that of being attacked and reacting without fear. At the Basic School we would often talk among ourselves about what we would really do if and when the shit hit the wall. Would we show courage or cowardice? Most of my classmates never were in a situation to find out, and most will never know. I KNOW. As the saying goes, I stared the ape in the eye and didn't back down. Now, again this is between you and me; I wouldn't share these feelings outside of family.

We got into single file and headed into the cornfield. We were a lot more alert and not wondering if we would be attacked, but when. By the way, the info for my medal had to be supplied by the CO. He certainly had his hands full at the time, and the fact that he recalled my actions with specificity told me he felt they were very significant towards preventing a major disaster with a lot of casualties.

60

From: Paden Waldruff
Date: January 3, 2009
To: Robert H. Waldruff

Dear Dad:

I am experiencing a rapid heartbeat and a few involuntary dots of water on my eyes.

Your strength has been a constant presence in my life. I wonder, did you have the same issues I did when you were growing up? What was your relationship like with your parents?

I've pondered for a moment, and I don't know how to say the following. So I guess I'll just say it. I envy the things you know about yourself after the challenges you faced in Vietnam. I assume it has shaped your life.

I am getting off point here. I am anxious for you to continue.

61

From: Robert H. Waldruff
Date: January 8, 2009
To: Paden Waldruff

Paden,

Since you are female and I a male, I don't think I had a lot of the same issues you had growing up! I was the middle child and did not want to make waves. I was however always seeking attention, as Sandy was the "princess" and Larry the "baby." That's probably what made me an overachiever, seeking to make my own mark. I did a lot of boyish mischievous things, but nothing horrible. I guess I was a pretty good kid.

My father was actually fearless when it came to getting done what he wanted to get done. No doubt you and I share this trait of being able to get things done. He would absolutely never take no for an answer, and he would not be intimidated by people or circumstances. He was a big dreamer; he shot for the moon. He fell short, but he was always in the game. He was also an optimist about life and America, and he truly believed he could accomplish anything he set out to do. Up until his last breath I'm sure he thought he would get back to the highway, get a ride, and get home safely. He had a lot of ups and downs, but would wake up every day and get back at it.

I guess I was pretty close to him. I forgave the disappointments and appreciated his work ethic and moral compass. I digress, as I could write a lot about our relationship. Mom was Mom, all bluster, soft as a marshmallow. Even without realizing it, we each knew she would throw herself under a bus if it meant saving our lives. She would fight for us at every turn, like a mama bear. Don't mess with her cubs!

I'm sure Vietnam changed me in a lot of ways, primarily on my values of what was really important and what was BS. Facing into the jaws of death tends to have that effect. Your comment of envy reminds me of Ronald Reagan's quote "Most men go through life wondering if they made a difference. Marines don't have that problem!"

We headed single file into the cornfield in the heat of the day. Our mission had now changed, as we were no longer providing security for villagers. I think our new mission was that we had located the enemy we were going to close with and destroy him. I'm sure that battalion command, knowing we were in the middle of a hornet's nest, saw an opportunity for a significant encounter and an opportunity to get some enemy kills.

The cornfield was typical, dense with tall stalks and visibility limited. We set on a course to bisect the field and exit at the far corner near the berm. That was where, a day earlier, the patrol and my artillery fire had come upon some VC. About halfway in, my radio operator with his radio had gotten too far behind me. He missed a zigzag by the column, and ventured off into the corn stalks. When I realized he had done this, I stopped and tried to get his attention. But he'd gone too far and out of sight. Years later I have laughed at this, but it was pretty serious at the time. I couldn't yell for him, as we didn't know how close Charles was. I headed into the stalks, sort of loudly whispering his name. Lucky for him, he circled back without getting lost and came up to me. Not wanting to further his embarrassment, I said we needed to get back to the column ASAP.

The column emerged from the cornfield and snaked through some elephant grass, a rice field, and into a Vietnamese cemetery. Vietnamese would bury their dead above ground and heap tall mounds of dirt on top of the corpse. I guess this was because if they buried them underground, the monsoon rains would eventually wash them up. This was where the CO decided to dig in for the night. As spooky as it sounds, I agreed it was the best spot. It was getting to dusk, and this was the only area clear enough for us to set up a perimeter defense. The platoon commanders split up the perimeter and had their Marines dig in for the night. The command group set up between two burial mounds and parked the Husky by one opening.

My radioman and I dug our fighting holes next to a mound,

and I targeted our command fires. These were pre-targeted trails, openings, etc. that would be likely entry routes for the enemy if they decided to attack us during the night. They were called in to the battery, pre-marked for fire, and given a target number like 1. Thus, if it hit the fan in the dark of night, I would and could not be looking at a map to call in a fire mission. I'd only have to say, "Target 1," and adjust the fire after the rounds hit.

We had a psych-ops unit with us (psychological warfare unit), and they set up their loud-speakers and started broadcasting in Vietnamese. They blared that the VC should surrender, lay down their arms, and seek amnesty (the Chieu Hoi program). They also made other anti-NVA comments, and talked of the futility of their cause. We also had a 60 millimeter mortar squad who set up their tubes and were firing at nearby suspected hiding places.

You get the picture. Here were a bunch of Marines desecrating a sacred burial ground, harassing the VC verbally with loud speakers, and mortaring the area. As night fell, the already highly motivated enemy was now extremely agitated and probably licking their chops for some payback. We were in the middle of a large number of enemy, and we certainly had accomplished our mission of encouraging a fight!

62

From: Paden Waldruff
Date: January 18, 2009
To: Robert H. Waldruff

Dear Dad:

Oh my God. Hang on, let me read it one more time. Oh my God.

A cemetery with mortar fire and loud speakers broadcasting all night.

Clearly our Vietnam narrative is at an apex, but I must also tell you that I truly appreciate hearing your thoughts on your relationship with your father.

I am as ready as I'll ever be to hear about what happened that night.

63

From: Robert H. Waldruff
Date: January 27, 2009
To: Paden Waldruff

Paden,

I want to spend a little time on military medals. All services award medals for heroic or meritorious service. In the Navy and USMC, the top award for heroic is the Medal of Honor, followed by the Navy Cross, Silver Star, and Bronze Star. The facts and circumstances of the "heroic" action dictates which award is given. The procedure is this—an eyewitness writes up the action in a report, it is sent up the chain of command and reviewed by several individuals who then determine if an award is merited, and which medal.

The Bronze Star is unique in that it can be awarded for heroic or meritorious. If awarded for heroic, the combat distinguishing device is authorized which is a "V" for valor worn on the medal and ribbon. Thus, when one says he has a Bronze Star, one is never sure if it was for heroic or meritorious. For example, Eric Sundin said his son, as well as most, received a Bronze Star for having completed a tour in Iraq. That would be for meritorious.

The Silver Star, Navy Cross, and obviously, the Medal of Honor are considered by most as pretty special. General Fegan once told me I deserved a Silver Star, but there was some technicality. General Fegan received two Silver Stars in his career. I never thought much of this, as I never felt what I did was out of the ordinary. As I've aged, I've come to think maybe I did something special and a Silver Star would have been special. All of this is just between us. I don't know if you heard Eric's comment about the Bronze Star, but he said anyone who gets one for Heroic should get the Silver Star!

Now the rest of this recollection is based on memory, conjecture, and things I heard later from various people.

We settled in for the night in our holes, expecting the worst. I dozed off. It appears Charles penetrated our perimeter and entered our position. A hell of a fight ensued as the Marines fought to expel the intruders.

I was hit with a lot of shrapnel from an RPG (rocket propelled grenade), which I'm sure also hit the Husky and sprayed hot metal in all directions. I remember feeling something hitting me in the gut, and a dull pain. I'm sure my body went into shock immediately.

All the while, I was in God's hands. I was maybe going to heaven, never to experience life again. I vividly remember total silence, and following that, a bright white light. This phenomenon has been described as a near-death experience. I've become fascinated with stories of other people's near-death experiences, and there is actually considerable scholarly research performed on this topic. I remember feeling calm. There was exquisite peace and relaxation, total quiet, and the bright white light. I have no idea how long this lasted but my number was not up.

As I slowly regained consciousness, I heard gunfire and the CO screaming to cease fire, cease fire. I felt fine and was searching for my weapon, talking to my radio operator to get on the radio for a fire mission. The CO yelled to the command group "Everybody okay?" I felt down and must have felt blood. Now since my intestines had been torn open and were exposed, and I had a scalp wound, I must have been quite a sight. The CO turned a flashlight on me. He saw I was in serious trouble and needed a medivac ASAP or would probably die from blood loss.

I was coherent and don't remember feeling pain. I listened to a radio operator call Marble Mountain for a Marine Helicopter medivac. I heard him tell the CO that because we were under attack, the Colonel felt it was too dangerous to send a chopper to our position. He feared it being shot down, thus losing both the bird and a Marine. I'll go to my grave feeling that even then, there was a pilot ready and not afraid. But the Colonel had to make the tough call. I heard the CO grab the phone and scream "I've got an officer down who needs a chopper right now to live!" I think this is when I started to get scared. For the first time I realized something very serious was going on.

As God is my witness, a guardian angel was there that hot morning of July 17, 1970. The radio operator yelled to the CO that an army warrant officer was flying a chopper close by. He had overheard our transmission, and said to give him our coordinates. He was coming to get me. Now, he could have kept flying to his base and not risked his life. No one would have known or blamed him. But no, he chose to fly into a small perimeter landing zone surrounded by VC, knowing his chopper was an inviting target and a sitting duck. This brave human being, forever unknown to me, SAVED MY LIFE.

While we waited, I told my radio operator to remember the pre-designated targets. I was carried to the landing zone in a poncho liner. While waiting, I screamed at the corpsman for morphine. I don't remember if I was even in pain. This was probably from my memory at TBS, that when one was seriously wounded morphine would deaden the pain. The corpsman told me I could not have it. I had an intestinal wound, and it would kill me.

The pain, the fear, the waiting, the helplessness culminated in my screaming out for help. I don't feel this was cowardice, under the circumstances. I have read many stories of men screaming out when seriously wounded. For many years afterward, I would awaken Mom with a guttural scream in the middle of the night. This has stopped, maybe in only the past eight to ten years. I imagine the scream was my subconscious remembering this event.

I calmed down and lay silent. I still vividly remember telling myself that I would not die in the dirt of this cemetery. I would live to see you and Mom. The mind is an awesome thing.

What seemed like forever ended with the sight and sound of the chopper landing. Flares had been lit. Once the chopper was on the ground, several of my fellow Marines carried me in the poncho to the back of the chopper. They set me down on the floor, ran out the back, and then screamed and waved to the pilot to "GO!" Slowly and loudly my savior expertly lifted the CH47 into the sky. We sped off to the 95th Medivac, an Army hospital unit in Da Nang.

At the time, I had a strange thought. I was thinking that I would receive a Purple Heart medal and would qualify for the Vietnam Meritorious Ribbon. You had to be in country for six months for that (and my tour would have only been five and a half) or wounded to qualify for it.

Several years later, I ran into a corporal while playing golf with General Fegan. He looked like he had seen a ghost. He said, "Sir, when you left in that chopper we thought you were dead!"

64

From: Paden Waldruff
Date: March 3, 2009
To: Robert H. Waldruff

Dear Dad:

Speechless.

I've been sitting on this for a while. It was unintentional, because current events have knocked me off my game. And also intentional, because I kept thinking the emotions I was having wouldn't translate into words.

One thing I know is that I owe that Army Warrant Officer more than I could ever define as well. He gave me my father. I feel so fortunate in this world to have the authentic and iconic image of a strong father. I feel so fortunate to know you as a person.

To add a little levity, an old friend and I have joked about our fathers for decades. She says the only direction I can go in relationships is down, and the only direction she can go is up.

I hope you feel like our exchange is far from finished. The more I read about Vietnam, the more I feel its present-day impact.

What happened when you got to Da Nang?

Love,

P

65

From: Paden Waldruff

Date: March 15, 2009

To: Anne F. Waldruff, Robert H. Waldruff

Subject: MOM, YOUR PERSPECTIVE IS VERY
IMPORTANT

Dear Mom:

YOUR ROLE WAS VERY IMPORTANT.

I recently watched a documentary that compared two things
that happened at the same time during Vietnam. One was a major
surprise battle with many army losses, and the other a protest at a
Wisconsin University.

Westmoreland was leading the effort, passing his orders down
to a guy named Hayes. Hayes was passing his orders down to a
young man named Allen.

Allen was a husband and a father of three young daughters. His
father was a General and Vietnam was young Allen's opportunity
to prove himself. There is early footage of the wedding and
commentary from the wife of how proud she was of her husband.
The future looked bright.

While Allen was in Vietnam, his wife wrote to him to let him know that she wanted a divorce. She had joined the anti-war movement, and said she couldn't love him knowing what he was doing.

I am sorry to get a bit maudlin here. A firsthand account from the battle said that the usually proactive Allen was paralyzed that day. His paralysis resulted in his death. He was staring at a picture of his daughters when it happened.

We will never know for sure what was going through Allen's mind that day. But you can't tell me that the role of loved ones stateside wasn't incredibly important.

66

From: Anne Waldruff

Date: March 15, 2009

To: Paden Waldruff

Dear Paden,

I will give you any memories, and they are vivid, of my time with you as a newborn. I'll also tell you about the year of taking care of Dad through the eleven surgeries he underwent.

Just got news that a friend over in Westham that her house burned down yesterday. We heard the fire trucks, and now they are asking for any pictures and memories I have. I taught all three children so I will go through my things to give them. One never knows.

Mom

67

From: Robert H. Waldruff

Date: March 16, 2009

To: Paden Waldruff

Paden,

No, not at all. As a matter of fact, we spent a lot of time with the Schmitts at Camp Lejeune. Surely you remember Jay Jay?

After I left the Corps and moved to Richmond, Ed Zeigler called repeatedly. Harry Tower would show up and call. I felt that part of my life was behind me and basically told both of them to buzz off. Ed did, as I've never heard from him again. Harry calls me every Marine Corps Birthday with a message. I've not called him back in several years.

Jeff never called. They did come through Richmond, though We went to dinner at the Ground Round over by Willow Lawn. You should remember that. I think Jeff felt as I did—move on.

Mom found Jeff and Linda's address in Raleigh, but no telephone number. You could write to him and ask if he's the Lieutenant who used to take a cab with me to Ishikawa, and drop beer off in the sugar cane to retrieve on the way back to the base! Jeff was with me pretty much most of the way: Fort Sill, Okinawa, First Marine Division, Da Nang, the Que Son Mountains, and Camp Lejeune.

As a matter of fact, we drove to Durham one night and went to a Duke/Virginia basketball game with Larry.

68

From: Robert H. Waldruff
Date: March 20, 2009
To: Paden Waldruff

Paden,

You're getting a little carried away. I did not save the world, or single-handedly win the war in Vietnam. I was on a dangerous mission with a company of Marines, and we encountered a lot of contact with the VC and NVA in the Northern Arizona. I did what I was trained to do by the finest military organization in the history of the world. I will go to my grave proud of the way I reacted under fire.

As my savior lifted off I do not know if we received enemy fire or not. We sure were a fine target. We made the trip to Da Nang in about twenty-thirty minutes, I would surmise. We hit the landing pad at the entrance to the 95th Medivac Hospital sometime in the middle of the night.

I was put on a gurney, and remember the two doctors looking me over and talking. They were obviously preparing me for triage. My surgeon I later learned was Dr. Mott. All USMC medical support is provided by Navy personnel, but this was an Army hospital. I was rolled into a large quonset hut that was the hospital, put under an anesthetic, and "patched-up" to become stabilized. They then prepared me for evacuation to the US for major rehab treatment.

I later learned that the doctors had removed my transverse colon and six feet of small intestine. They performed a double-barreled colostomy, and cauterized me with a tube through my nose.

I also had what turned out to be a superficial scalp wound, which was bleeding a lot. Everybody was initially concerned that perhaps I had a concussion and/or brain damage. They could not perform any tests until I regained consciousness. I also had part of my ear shot off, and several smaller wounds on my arm and leg. I had lost a lot of blood. I think I needed eight pints in all to replace the loss.

Sometime the next day, I woke up in a bed in intensive care, under a sheet, with no clothes. I had a blood transfusion running into one arm, and a plasma transfusion in the other arm. My first feeling was of relief that I had survived, and that I had my arms and legs attached. I looked under the sheet and wasn't sure what was going on! I saw a lot of open wounds, and colostomy bags on each side.

I don't know how long it was before Dr. Mott arrived. When he did, he brought me up to date on everything that was going on with my body. He told me that if everything went okay, I would probably be stabilized and sent to a naval hospital in Japan for another week, and then sent to the US.

They wheeled me down to a room to run some scans on my head and brain. The scans indicated that other than my being a crazy Marine, everything was normal. I had around-the-clock attention from the nursing staff. They were constantly changing my colostomy bags and replacing empty blood and plasma containers with fresh ones. These were wonderful women—very professional, caring, and compassionate. They were more forgotten, great, and courageous Americans.

The second day the Commandant of the Marine Corps, General Leonard F. Chapman, and the Assistant Commandant, who were in Vietnam for an update, visited the hospital. They came to award me my Purple Heart, which General Chapman pinned to my sheet. General Chapman was one of General Fegan's favorites. The generals made a few comments, answered by a lot of "Yes, Sir" congratulated me, and left. I later learned the Generals had their own communication network. My condition and progress were relayed back to General Fegan outside normal channels.

By the way, Grans told us she was awakened in the night at the exact time I was wounded. Who knows; the psyche is amazing. Also, you all found out as you were staying at the General Officers beach cottage at Camp Lejeune. The base executive officer, a colonel, came out to give General Fegan the news. This was probably not what the Colonel wanted to be doing. The best anyone knew at this time, I was seriously wounded in the abdomen and extremities with possible serious head wounds. But, I was alive.

Grandma and Grandpa got a telegram and a call from General Fegan. I can only imagine they were terrified, expecting the worst, and helpless, hoping for more and better news. Sandy and John were at church and an usher came to her and said she had a very important phone call. It was Martha calling about the news. Sandy claims she turned to John and said "It's Bobby!"

I'm sure this early phase was a lot harder for you all than for me. I knew what was going on, and you all had nothing but fear and uncertainty. Again, this is something Mom's not talked to me much about. What were her thoughts, fears, prayers? She was only twenty-four, with a baby, and a husband 7,000 miles away, maybe lying dying in a hospital!

The third day, Dr. Mott came to my bed with an assistant to check me out. My "only problem" was a lingering fever due to infection. Infection in Vietnam was always a big fear. He pulled out my catheter tube and said, "Oh well, here goes." It was fine, as I could urinate under my own steam.

I was wheeled out of intensive care, and into the main patient room. This was in the center of the quonset hut and had two long rows of beds.

I've always loved the show M*A*S*H for it's wit and humor. Its set was very similar to what I experienced at the 95th.

69

From: Paden Waldruff
Date: April 26, 2009
To: Robert H. Waldruff

Dear Dad:

So many thoughts attached to every email you send me.

I must admit that during my first read through, I typically have my mouth open and am trying to form the word "What?" This reaction represents the full range of emotions I am feeling. I can't stop my mind from flashing back to my life with you. Having this new knowledge places a new and important layer on all of my memories.

On my second read-through, I am always taken aback and proud of your thoughts and concerns for your family and your country.

I am so grateful to be able to learn more about you and your life.

And in a larger sense, I think what we are doing here is very important.

You know that I've become a student of Vietnam documentaries and interviews with soldiers. They describe their experiences and how their lives have been impacted. Almost universally, the first-person accounts are used to prove the conclusion that the US is a selfish, impetuous, imperialist nation that absolutely ruined the lives of all who served, drafted or not, wounded or not. At this point, I can almost feel the heart of the "documentarist" beating faster when a decorated officer sheds a tear of shame for the camera.

For those of my generation and younger who even bother to take the time to study history, these pieces create fact. What percentage of viewers born in the 1960s and later stops to wonder about who is so readily willing to be interviewed over and over again for these films and what their agenda might be?

I think what I know, and am continuing to learn, about you and men like you is very important. I know that I was born in 1970, shortly before you were severely wounded in service to your country in Vietnam. I can also attest to the fact that I have no memory of your experience in Vietnam having any impact on my childhood, other than making me proud of you and my country.

Please continue.

70

From: Robert H. Waldruff
Date: May 8, 2009
To: Paden Waldruff

Paden,

Remember that, regarding the soldiers who seemed so willing and eager to criticize the US Vietnam policy, there were the political activists, e.g. John Kerry. But, because a lot of the soldiers were draftees, a lot of them were forced to serve against their will. They were probably losers anyway, and had chips on their shoulders. Morale got so bad in the Army that often the enlisted men would throw hand grenades into their officer's quarters to kill them. These were called "fraggings."

Vietnam made the case to do away with the draft. We did, much to the better for the country. You don't see many soldiers or Marines who served in Iraq or Afghanistan doing "I hate America" interviews. They chose to serve of their own volition. This is another reason I think the Marines have historically had more esprit de corps. They have almost always been an all-volunteer service except for a couple of years during Vietnam when the Marines did use the draft.

I spent about a week in the 95th Medivac Hospital. I was 100 percent bed-ridden, and had a rubber mat filled with ice water under me at all times to try and break the fever.

A rather interesting and wild visit I had was with Brigadier General Simmons. He was sort of the Marine Corps historian. He knew a lot of details and individuals, and of course knew all about your grandfather and his father. He explained during our conversation that forty-eight hours earlier he had been a guest at a dinner party hosted by General and Mrs. Fegan. Mom was his assigned dinner partner. Now, here I was, just out of the jungle, talking to a man who had just been with Mom—quite a juxtaposition. It was interesting to talk with him. It felt good hearing first hand all about Mom.

One of the best nurses I had, as I found out from another nurse, was a former VC sympathizer who had served in a NVA hospital. She apparently got fed up with their treatment of their wounded and defected.

I slept a lot, and received blood transfusions around the clock. I don't recall feeling much pain, but I was receiving pain-killing shots which felt "fabulous." As a matter of fact, too fabulous.

I learned when I got back to the states—I think it was from the corporal I ran into at the golf course who had been with I Company the night of action—that the next day the Company abandoned the mission and returned to Hill 55. This was probably because someone realized there were more bad guys out there than they thought. The Company was without its FO, and they probably didn't want to risk more casualties.

I learned more from a USMC history of the 5th Marines book which I got about three or four years ago. The week after I Company returned to Hill 65, July 24, 1970, the Marines returned to the cornfields of My Hiep with tanks and amtracs. They leveled the entire field, destroying over 30,000 bushels of corn. If the civilians couldn't harvest this crop, then we sure weren't going to let the VC and NVA harvest it!

The hospital was pretty full, and there were several Marines suffering from severe burn wounds. It was a pretty awful sight watching them receive treatment. On July, 24th, 1970, I was transported down to the airfield, boarded a cargo plane, and was flown to Yokosuka naval base. I was placed in the Naval hospital for more stabilization and relaxation before flying home.

This is the same base where we Marine officers stationed at Mt. Fuji had gone for a night out at the officers club for dinner and "some" drinks. We had managed to get totally drunk and out of control. It was when we lost track of my man Lt. Bob Brown, he of four Purple Hearts fame. We had found him hours later passed out in a bathroom stall. We had somehow got to our rooms and passed out for the rest of the night. That was probably only four months earlier. As you've read, it was quite a four months for RHW.

The Readers were stationed at this base. Jim Reader was a

colonel, and they were longtime friends of the Fegans. Mrs. Reader did volunteer work at the hospital and met the wounded as we were helicoptered into the base from the airport. She waited with us under some shade trees until we were transported to the Hospital. She was fabulous, and it was great talking to someone so knowledgeable of the Fegans. I don't know if you remember, but we ran into them years later at Topsail Beach. They owned a beach house on the Inlet side of the Island. They had a daughter with a funny but cool name, who was off to Princeton I believe when we visited them.

Also, during the time I was at the Hospital, Pete Gray arrived in a coma. Remember I mentioned him earlier—a UVA guy who was sharp, from Richmond, and was president of the college his 4th year. I never saw him, but he died in intensive care. When the Commandant had visited, Recon put on a display of how Marines would insert into the jungle by rappelling down ropes from helicopters. During Pete's drop there was a horrible miscommunication. The pilot thought Pete was off the rope and on the ground, but he was not. He was dragged, caught in the rope, through the tops of trees. By the time they got him off the rope, he was unconscious and never regained consciousness. A horrible, horrible event. Years ago his family started the Pete Gray Foundation at UVA. It's since been renamed the Gray-Carrington Foundation. I've been a contributor every year.

I celebrated my 26th Birthday in this hospital, a funny story. It seems Aunt Lou, unbeknownst to me, mailed me a birthday ribbon cake to Vietnam. She mailed it plenty early to be sure that I would receive it. Well, as events occurred, that poor cake went to Hill 52, Hill 55, the 95th Medivac. It finally caught up to me on my actual birthday in Japan. Needless to say, there wasn't much left of the cake, and what was left was unsuitable for eating. We got a big laugh out of it at the Hospital, and it became a family story.

While in Japan, a Marine Gunnery Sgt. Defazio stationed in the US, without General Fegan's knowledge and/or permission, took it upon himself to hook up conference calls with Grandma and Grandpa on one line and Grans, BaBa and Mom on the other line. It was rather awkward to say the least. "Bob, how are you?" "Ah, I'm feeling okay. How are you? Is Paden okay?" When do you think you'll fly home?" "Don't know for sure." etc ..., etc ...

So, by the time I was 26 I had gotten married, had a daughter, graduated with an MBA from the University of Chicago, had seen combat in Vietnam as a Marine Lieutenant, and survived an NVA attack and a critical wound. And people wonder why I have no patience for a lot of the self-indulgent immature behavior of the young people of today!

71

From: Paden Waldruff
Date: June 21, 2009
To: Robert H. Waldruff

Dear Dad:

Happy Father's Day, Dad.

I am so grateful for you and our relationship. It means the world to me to know you as a father, man, and friend. I am beyond proud to be your daughter, and it feels so good to know that you know everyday how much I love you.

Not to go overboard, but God bless you for serving when called, and God bless everyone who was with you along the way.

I can't imagine how weird it was to have the conversation with Brigadier General Simmons. Things have changed so much for deployed soldiers in terms of technology, enabling them to stay in touch with their loved ones. That it is hard for me to wrap my mind around, how separated you and Mom were. I think the question on my mind is twofold or maybe threefold.

1) I respect the practice of Generals coming to Vietnam to show support for the wounded. I would think that the gesture would be

very meaningful. Was it?

2) I would guess, but I'm not entirely sure, that Mom would have spoken pretty honestly with Simmons over the course of the evening about how she was feeling. I am sure she was super worried about you, and scared. When Simmons talked to you, did you feel like he was speaking as a professional or did he speak to you man-to-man?

3) My impression is that General Fegan didn't fully accept your marriage to his daughter, which had to have been really hard for you. If I am correct, was that information common knowledge? I would guess the answer would be no among the Marines in service, but possibly yes among the generals. Did having a powerful father-in-law leave you in a weird position with your peers? You never mention it. You mention the brotherhood that you felt with your peers. As always, I respect how you choose to place your focus.

Yes, I remember the Reader's beach house very clearly. That visit is one of the few memories I have of Vietnam being discussed. My memory is of Mrs. Reader being presented as an important woman, who was with you when you were hurt. I remember the daughter, too. I don't know how to spell her name, but I remember they said "Aynnes." She took Tucker and me out onto their screened-in porch on the back of the house while the adults were inside talking. There were tons of shells and shark teeth they had collected on the beach. She let us each pick a tooth to keep. She was very kind to us, and we were enchanted.

I appreciate knowing that the Marines returned to that cornfield and finished the job.

My heart breaks with each story you tell me of a man who didn't return home to his family. In addition, I feel pretty close to physically ill when I think of how our country responded to the brave men who served.

Thank God my father came home. You shouldn't have patience for a lot of the self-indulgent immature behavior of the young and older people of today. It will be our downfall.

What happened when you left Japan?

72

From: Robert H. Waldruff
Date: July 27, 2009
To: Paden Waldruff

Paden,

You do have a knack of getting to the nub of things. Yes, both Grans and BaBa were strongly against my marriage to Mom. When we were dating in college, Renny would park his car a block away, and Mom would meet us to avoid my meeting the folks. I don't think I was too terribly riled-up by this, as we kind of blew them off as being out-of-touch, overly strict, parents. As our relationship got more serious during the summer of 1966, I did have an occasional cocktail and cookout dinner with BaBa and Max. I was off to U of C, Mom was off to MWC for her senior year, and Colonel Fegan was off to Vietnam. They were of course always polite and cordial, but it was always obvious that I was not their choice for Mom. What he told his Marine pals I can only guess, but I imagine at best it was not complimentary.

Now I'm sure at this time the last thing he or I ever thought was that he would end up a Lt. General and I would receive a medal for heroic achievement and a Purple Heart as a Marine 1st Lieutenant in Vietnam. He was, and always was, in his Marine world with little tolerance for non-Marines. I'm sure he always thought Mom would marry a Marine and carry on as a Marine Corps wife. His worst nightmare was Mom marrying someone who did not seem to want to serve his country. That was probably his conclusion about me, without my input. He may have dwelled on me going to graduate school without any means of financial support except Mom's teaching job. He may have thought that I was a draft-dodger, hanging out in graduate school with the rest of the draft dodgers, making Mom work to pay the bills. You can just imagine some of the wisecracks when the Fegans were at parties and their friends would ask, "How's Anne these days?"

There's the infamous story of Nina Platt and Grans taking Mom and Joanne to lunch, offering to get them dates with some handsome Marine Corps Captains. That is, dump Bob. To my knowledge the only Marine that stood up for me was Bob Bohn, a retired Major General. He was a longtime friend of BaBa's, and did some pretty heroic stuff in Korea. After talking with me, he told BaBa and Max that he thought I was smart, had my head on straight, and that U of C was a fabulous school. He said that I would make a great husband for Mom. He was the one who recommended that we honeymoon in Antigua.

We got engaged in the parking lot of O'Hare field in February 1967, much to the chagrin of the Fegans. I'm sure they were hoping that once I went off to Chicago and Mom got back to MWC, our relationship would fade. When I asked Grans for Mom's hand, she requested we not marry until BaBa returned from Vietnam in August 1967. I said absolutely. My "reward" was that as BaBa walked Mom down the aisle at our wedding, he tried to bribe her with a free trip to Spain if she would call the whole thing off! Of course, at the wedding and reception were all the Fegans' Marine friends. They had obviously been "influenced" with misinformation prior to meeting me. I never dwelled on all this, as I never doubted Mom's love. Actually, all this probably made our resolve stronger. We immediately left Falls Church to set up our life together in Chicago. This turned out to have many enduring benefits.

You may remember the Houghtons, who retired in La Jolla. They always had us over for drinks when you and Tucker came with us to San Diego. They were always exceptionally nice to us. I think it was their way of saying that they couldn't believe what the Fegans put Mom and me through. General Houghton, by the way, was stationed in Hawaii when I was wounded. He was in command of Vietnam forces, and took a personal interest in my well-being. He even lobbied to get me a Silver Star. Whenever we saw him, he treated me like a wounded war hero, with almost embarrassing respect.

BaBa never confided much in me. After I returned from Vietnam, I think our relationship was one of mutual respect. They took very good care of you and Mom during my absence. Our families spent a lot of time together, and I think grew to enjoy each other's company. No doubt, my Marine Corps experience enhanced our communication. He never mentioned his "treatment" of me in the early years, and there was no reason he should. He did tell me one time when we were alone that due to my actions in Vietnam, I had joined a very exclusive Marine Corps club. This caught me by surprise, and has become more meaningful to me each year. No, BaBa never did anything devious or mean to me. I'm sure he was making the best decisions for his family as he could at the time. I represented a total unknown, who was taking Mom away to a world he knew nothing about. I've wondered if any of his buddies, after my wound, ever chided him with "Well, Joe, I guess you didn't know your ass from a hole in the ground about your son-in-law!" General Simmons chatted me up as a Marine superior officer, but also as a man with a sincere interest in my well-being.

As far as my relationship with my peers—them knowing that my father-in-law was a General—I don't think it ever mattered. They could readily see that I got no special treatment, and that I had to go through the same Marine training as everyone else. We were young, macho, doing our thing, and all in the same boat. As my career changed after Vietnam, several of my superior officers—not my peers—would treat me as a little special. It was nothing significant, but guess they thought it might help to keep their careers on track. Little did they know my opinion of other officers was rarely requested, and I'm certain it never influenced General

Fegan's decisions.

When I was out of the hospital and easing back into Marine life, I had an office job for eight months, working directly for a Major and a Colonel. One morning General Fegan notified me that I'd be going with him and his staff to observe a training exercise in Vieques, Puerto Rico. He said not to worry about the Major and Colonel, that he'd let them know. We had a great trip. When I went back to work, the Major was livid and pissed-off. The Colonel was fine. I shared this with General Fegan, and he essentially said not to sweat the Major! I think all of this stuff was a big part of why Grans would always say that I joined the Marines to please them. Nothing could be farther from the truth, but it turned out to be one of many benefits of my decision.

I left Yokosuka Naval Hospital for Camp Lejeune on July 29, 1970, on an Air Force plane full of wounded Marines and soldiers. The Air Force nurse was rather mean—the only one I ever met who had a problem with me. When I asked her for a pan in which to relieve myself, she told me to get up and go to the toilet myself. Well, I had not left my cot since I was wounded, and I had IVs in both arms. I said to myself, "OK, lady, here goes ... and you better hope I make it!"

We landed at Edwards AFB; it was near 29 Palms, but it's no longer there. We were put on different planes to be flown to our final destinations. As the cargo door opened, there was almost no one there, only three elderly ladies. They walked around to each of us, handed us a tiny American Flag, and said "Thank you for your sacrifice." I flew to Huntsville AFB in Alabama, watched the college all-star football game, and went to sleep.

The next day, August 1, 1970, I flew on a small plane to Cherry Point Marine Air Base, Cherry Point, NC. I was put into an ambulance, and driven the 50 miles to Camp Lejeune Naval Hospital. Grans, Mom, and BaBa met me there, and walked with me as I was wheeled into my hospital room. You were not there. Mom wasn't sure what to expect, and didn't want to cause any unnecessary confusion. We made small talk and met my doctor, Commander George Frankhouser. He was another savior and lucky blessing on my journey. We all agreed I should get some rest, and set a time to bring you over to see me the next day.

June 6 to August 1, 1970—fifty-seven days—what a trip!

73

From: Paden Waldruff

Date: July 27, 2009

To: Robert H. Waldruff

Dear Dad:

I am on the edge of my seat for day 58 and beyond.

I love you Dad,

P

74

From: Robert H. Waldruff
Date: October 10, 2009
To: Paden Waldruff

Paden,

August 2, 1970, was a Sunday. Mom, you, and General and Mrs. Fegan all came by to check in. I don't remember much. I'm sure there was a lot of small talk and a lot of talking and looking at you. All kind of like the Henry routine. Grandma and Grandpa came about a week later, and stayed for about three or four days. I'm sure this was awkward for everybody, as BaBa and Grans and their world could not have been any more foreign. Grandma and Grandpa came to see me several times, but I remember very little of what was said. During their visit I had my first of four major operations on my road to recovery.

The first operation was scraping a thin layer of skin from my thigh. You can still see the spot. This skin was grafted over the open hole in my abdomen, and also over the pie-shaped hole in my ear lobe. This left me in considerable pain, more than any of the other operations. I'm sure that I wasn't much company for my parents, and my condition probably worried them.

During most of August, I continued to have IVs of fluid pumped into my body, and of course had my two "friends" the colostomy bags. The rehab plan was to stabilize my body, cure any infection, let all my organs "calm down" get my strength up, and then open up my intestines. This would be to reconnect the two ends where my transverse colon had been. They'd sew up the colostomy holes, and hope everything would start to work properly.

My doctor/surgeon/therapist/psychologist was Navy Commander, Dr. George Frankhouser. George went to Virginia Tech and UVA Med School. Not only was he a skilled surgeon, he was a master of understanding my psyche and emotions. I was in uncharted waters, was helpless and dependent, but I needed dignity and a sense of self-dependence. George was able to guide me through this seeming paradox. He was fabulous behind the scenes with Mom.

Mom and I have not talked much of this, the only time in my life when I was not in control. Mom said it was difficult for her, as I became withdrawn and sometimes selfish. After about a month, George told Mom to get me home. He said this would be the best therapy, even if it slowed down the medical rehab schedule.

This was when, as a gift from Martha, we acquired Emily. I will never forget after the first night I tried to return her. I did not, but only because the owner would not give me a refund! Our family now knows the emotional value of having pets. Emily was fantastic therapy as we bonded during our walks. She gave me a purpose, and asked for nothing in return. She was my friend. Of course, you and Mom also gave me plenty of love and attention. In a lot of ways, I've thought this down time was a fantastic gift. I got to spend quality time with you both. If I had not been wounded, I would probably have been off on some Marine training expedition.

We lived in a two-bedroom two-floor townhouse apartment that Mom had moved to during my WESTPAC tour. It was roomy and perfect for all of us. This was where you would persistently and defiantly get around the guard gate and crawl up the stairs, knowing we would have to get you and carry you down. Later, you would get out of your crib when you should have been asleep, and crawl down the steps to "surprise" us. We spent a lot of time with the Fegans. We had dinner at the General's quarters two or three times a week, afterwards strolling around the neighborhood showing you off.

The colostomy bags were awful. Since my intestines were "untrained", they would empty at all different times during the day and night without warning. This was embarrassing and annoying. They had to be constantly changed. This gave me insight about and appreciation for all the people in the world who have this condition permanently.

During this period I would go back to the hospital for major and minor operations, and stay anywhere from three days to a week and a half. During one stay in October, I was told to get shaped up, as General Fegan was coming by in an official capacity. When he and his aide arrived, Mrs. Fegan, Mom, and you were in tow. I was told I was being awarded a medal. My thought was, "Oh my God. I did nothing worthy of a medal. I'm receiving this only because General Fegan is my father-in-law."

I should have given the integrity of the Marine Corps more credit. But I kept thinking that the night of my wound, I really did nothing special. It turns out that it was for the day before, when we were attacked and I called in mortars and artillery.

It was several years before I reconciled with, accepted, and felt honored to have been awarded the Bronze Star with Combat V for heroic achievement in the Republic of South Vietnam.

75

From: Paden Waldruff
Date: December 5, 2009
To: Robert H. Waldruff

It has been a while since you sent me an update on our story. I didn't want to ask, but I was worried you felt we were finished. I was in the desert after everyone had gone to bed when I read the email below for the first time. I was so relieved (can't think of a more appropriate word) that you were willing to continue. Thank you.

After the first read, what struck me was that I know the spot well on your thigh where the skin graft was taken. I still can't believe, but am immensely proud of, the personal/physical sacrifices you've made for your country. I wish I could shake Dr. Frankhouser's hand. I never knew that Chief gave you Emily.

Five or six (or twenty) more readings before I got home. I think about what I'm learning from you. Learning from you, learning about myself, learning about people, learning about life. You need to be in control as it seems genetically encrypted and evidenced that things get done under your watch.

Let me restate on what I consider to be an objective platform, you are a war hero and a role model for the United States of America. Period. I detest the way certain politicians and parts of society have weighed in on those who bravely served in Vietnam.

It is my profound honor and privilege to interject into a conversation whenever I can, that my father served his country. It is regularly a surprise. Tucker and I are so "normal with the Waldruff twist" that those who know you think you are so "normal with the Waldruff twist." Yup, I always get to say, "the majority of the men who served did their duty, absorbed the personal consequences, and moved on with their lives."

Could you please pick up where you left off?

All my love,

P

76

From: Robert H. Waldruff
Date: January 14, 2010
To: Paden Waldruff

Paden,

We've not talked, but I know you to be a pensive person on important issues. Marking your body for life is certainly an important issue! So, I know your decision was not spontaneous.

You weren't drunk in some bar in Tijuana where your drinking buddies dared you to get a "tat." That is why most Marines have tattoos. No, you gave the decision considerable thought.

When I first saw it, I felt like I did when I received my Bronze Star. I don't deserve this recognition. I quickly realized it was not just about me, but the much bigger issue of the hundreds of thousands of men and women who risked it all for the love of country and a profound sense of responsibility.

I am humbled and honored, and I thank you for this eternal recognition of the good fight made by me and my band of brothers.

Love,
Dad

77

From: Paden Waldruff

Date: January 18, 2010

To: Robert H. Waldruff

Dear Dad:

I remain perplexed by your sentiment that you are undeserving of heroic recognition for your service to your country. In Vietnam, and in your life following.

Then I take a step back to think about what is genetically encrypted in me. I think I get it on a much smaller scale. I know I have not yet been truly tested. But on my small scale, I have a sense of duty that I must follow. I am proud/glad for it.

Yes, we all know that I screwed up and unintentionally did everything I could to ruin your and Mom's life when I was a teenager. Let's put that aside for the moment.

My sense of duty and responsibility have led to a firm that is now ten years old. I am 39, and I am looking for it to last for the rest of my career. And I run it with my family, which is in itself pretty freaking special. When I get an unusual and unexpected thank you from clients and the community for the work we do, I am mortified.

You are correct, marking my body for life was no small decision. And I waited years to tell you and Mom. I wasn't sure if I would tell you one day about it. If it were not for the 2009 Tea Party Protest on 9/12, I might never have said anything.

The day that I called you from Long Beach to make sure I didn't have a typo on my body for life was special. I am proud of my father. You never asked to be a representative of something that was out of your hands.

In addition to your military service, you represent capitalism. I am shocked by the assault on capitalism during my short life. So, you, in your life's work, are a hero to me on many fronts. That is what the ink means to me.

All of my love,

P

78

From: Robert H. Waldruff
Date: February 8, 2010
To: Paden Waldruff

Paden,

The fall of 1970 included time in and out of the hospital, and time at our Camp Lejeune apartment in Jacksonville with you, Mom, and Emily. We took a trip to DC to see Aunt Lou, and spent a couple days at Mary Ober's farm in Orange. Aunt Lou was in her glory, showing us all off and especially her wounded "son." She made a science of shopping around Alexandria and Orange for the "perfect" colostomy bags. It seems she was an expert, as several of her older friends had colostomies. Of course, Aunt Lou was an expert on almost everything.

I remember getting several phone calls from UVA Pika fraternity brothers, Renny Barnes, etc ... I'm sure these calls were well-intended and I was certainly thankful and polite to all callers. But I remember not really wanting to talk much, as how could they understand? Martha always said Vietnam changed me. Well of course it did, as it did everyone else, especially those

Marines involved in combat. She said I became withdrawn. I think she interpreted my reluctance to talk about Vietnam as being withdrawn. I think it was because I just didn't feel anyone could truly understand. I wanted to move on. I had been there, done that.

Dr. Frankhouser scheduled what we hoped would be my final operation, for the week after New Year's.

Shirley Wood said she wanted to come to Lejeune and see us for Christmas and before my operation. She did, and we had a New Year's Eve dinner party in her honor. We had several of the old Basic School classmates over for it. I have a picture of us lined up with our dinner plates at the apartment. In retrospect, I suspect Shirley was going through an incredible adjustment period. She was confused and lost, and was still clinging to Bob's memory. She may have felt that this was some kind of therapy to be with Marine friends who understood on a different level than her friends and family in Texas. I also think she came out of genuine concern for me and Mom.

Whe—what a time! It was lucky we were all young or we would have sat around crying!

We went to the hospital around seven p.m. for prepping, and kick-off was to be eight a.m. I was getting pretty used to this routine, including my pain shot to get me through the night.

As a final prep during December, Dr. Frankhouser, being always the thorough and cautious surgeon, wanted to be sure my intestines were clear and clean of any blockage. This included several barium enemas with X-rays and proctological exams. As a final check he wanted me to give myself a full enema at home, which should have been very routine since my intestines were not connected and stuff was flowing through them all the time. Well, after I gave myself the enema I started to feel tremendous pressure as though I was having a bowel movement. You said you wanted to hear the story! This was impossible, since I couldn't have a bowel movement.

I went to the hospital the next day, and George checked me out with his rubber glove and hand. It seems a chunk of C-rations, my "last supper" at My Diep, had gotten caught after my colon was removed and had gone undetected. Dr. Frankhouser then "performed surgery" by having me bend over. Using his hand, he went up my anal cavity and pulled out the C-ration pieces. This procedure was an utter joy to us both, and is one of those things that bonds physician and patient. He told me I had as similar an experience to a woman delivering a baby as any man could have!

The surgery was as successful as could be expected, and I had two days in intensive care. The worst part was that I had to cough every four or five hours to be sure to keep phlegm from collecting in my lungs. This was pretty painful against my newly acquired stitches. I was released on the fourth day. Now the key was to have a bowel movement, to be sure roughage could move through my intestines past where they were surgically connected. Around 6 p.m. on the sixth day, it happened. This was to the utter relief and joy of myself and Mom. It made me really appreciate the small things in life!

In February, I got my stitches removed and began about three more months of at-home recuperation. I believe it was in May 1971 that I was cleared for temporary duty. I was assigned a desk job at Headquarters 2nd Marine Division. That November, General Fegan and Grans left for Okinawa where he was to assume command of the 3rd Marine Division. Before he left, they were in temporary quarters, and they invited us over. They gave us a gift of $1,000, which got us out of debt. It was very considerate, and I never forgot it. In 1971 we moved onto the base and into officers quarters, leaving our apartment and all the memories.

Dr. Frankhouser, by the way, retired in Tappahannock. For a while I thought I'd go see him, to once again thank him. Then I thought, why bother him. I'm sure he'd moved on.

79

From: Robert H. Waldruff
Date: February 25, 2010
To: Paden Waldruff

Paden,

As we've discussed, it's an impossible task, even for the most objective person, to capture the true essence of serving in Vietnam on film. Combine that reality with the fact that Hollywood is anything but objective, and you get some pretty ridiculous stuff.

Most people think *Platoon* was the best and most realistic film about Vietnam. I actually enjoyed *Full Metal Jacket*, mostly for the boot camp part. But the film was pretty realistic, especially because the actor playing the DI was in fact a former Marine Drill Instructor. I also liked *Apocalypse Now*. Brando and Duval were excellent, even though the movie had nothing to do with Vietnam! Probably, each of these films had bits and pieces of reality.

My Marine nickname was "Gunner." I got this nickname in OCS, during the first couple of weeks. We candidates were trying to get our bearings and sort things out. The DIs were doing everything in their power to keep us off balance. We would have daily formations in front of the barracks, and this Gunnery Sergeant would shout at us to form into platoons. He was about five foot two, with this really deep and distinctive voice as he shouted at us to "Move! Move!"

During lights out, we laid in our bunks thinking aloud about what we had gotten ourselves into. A couple guys made some comments about the daily routine. I started shouting out and mimicking the voice of the preposterous Gunnery Sergeant. Well, this surprised everyone, and everyone broke up laughing. It was comic relief, and it reinforced that we were not insane. It showed we all had similar feelings about the goings-on. Well, I became known as "Gunner" and it stuck. Yes, I would say most Marines had nicknames.

80

From: Paden Waldruff

Date: March 21, 2010

To: Robert H. Waldruff

Dear Dad:

Wow. The 80s Army ad comes to mind, "We do more before 9 a.m. than most people do all day." You and Mom experienced so much by 1971. Your strength and desire to keep moving forward has always been an inspiration to me.

You were cleared for temporary duty in 1971. I know that my brother shares my birthplace. I have always been curious about what happened between your return from Vietnam in 1970 and Tucker's birth on September 6, 1972, and the day we left Camp Lejeune.

I really wish Aunt Lou and I could meet each other now. You, she and I could get into a great debate. I really wish I could hear her side of the story in the 2010 backdrop. Would she be horrified? Would she have crossed lines and become a Tea Party member? She was a woman who HAD to work, right?

Dr. Frankhouser—do you know his first name? I Googled him.

There is a Dr. Frank Houser that takes up most of the hits. I added Tappahannock to the search, with no clarity. I would never make a move without your consent, but I would love to thank the man or his family for his care of my wounded father.

Also—the army cowboy. Is there any way we could ever find out who he is? I am as committed to privacy and to constantly moving forward with life as you are. But I also think about how meaningful the postings are to you that you find on the internet.

81

From: Robert H. Waldruff
Date: August 2, 2010
To: Paden Waldruff

Paden:

When you asked me two years ago to share with you my (and Mom's) Vietnam story, I had no idea where it would lead and what would be our individual and collective reaction. I sensed the story was important to you, and I'm not surprised. What has surprised me is that the story was important to me, too, not in factual content—obviously important to me—but in sharing it with you. It puts a whole different perspective on the tale.

Whenever I read a note from a daughter of a fallen hero listed on The Black Wall Of Death, I get misty-eyed. That could have been you, and we would never have gotten to share our lives. The single most important fact is that I never really realized how lucky I was to have survived. It puts a whole lot of shit into perspective.

I appreciate your reference to me as a hero (although I'm not, and did not perform any acts of heroism), but the main thing is that I did survive. As Sergeant Major Alan Farrell says, "there's the by-God Glory!" My family and I have been blessed by the grace of God! Hold close that which you know to be true, and never stop searching for the truth.

Love,
Your Father

ADDENDUM

In the fall of 2016 I participated in a ten-week creative writing class for veterans taught by VCU writing professor and noted novelist, David L. Robbins. Robbins launched this initiative in early 2015 in conjunction with the Virginia War Memorial. It's called the Mighty Pen Project and is missioned to coax veterans to write stories of their individual experiences.

Honored by his leadership, guidance, writing skills, and passion, cocooned with other like minded veterans, I explored my inner composition and submitted four short stories for class criticism and reaction. These stories follow.

On the porch of our farm, Annie Oaks, with Matt Farrell's Enfield rifle.

ONE ACT PLAY

GUARDIAN ANGELS

A One-Act Play
By Robert Waldruff

World premiere September 2021,
Firehouse Theatre, Richmond, VA

CHARACTER	DESCRIPTION	AGE
Lieutenant	Marine artillery observer	25-28
Woman In White/Nurse/Wife	Spirit/Marine Nurse/Wife	25-28
Captain	Marine Combat Officer	30-35
Corpsman	Marine Combat Medic	20-30
Gunny	Marine Gunnery Sergeant	25-40
Chaplain	Marine Chaplain	40-50
Doctor Mott	Chief Surgeon	30-40
PA	Physician Associate	30-40
Major	Marine Casualty Officer	39-40

SCENE 1

(Brilliant white background funneled towards Woman In White;
enter Marine Lieutenant in combat gear)

LIEUTENANT

I have to go.

WOMAN IN WHITE

Stay.

LIEUTENANT

I don't think I can.

WOMAN IN WHITE

Stay.

(White light dims, battlefield scene comes alive, Lieutenant, wounded, lies on back, Woman In White remains, watching)

(Lieutenant suddenly sits up, grabs mouth to muffle a scream)

(Battle sounds: shouts, tracer rounds, mortar and grenades, Vietnamese shouting from loudspeakers; red flickers from flares overhead)

(Noise quiets)

GUNNY

Captain, we've pushed them back.

CAPTAIN

Cease fire! Cease fire! Anybody hit?

LIEUTENANT

(Grabs gut)

I think I am.

GUNNY

(Shines flashlight)

Good God. Corpsman up! Skipper, call a medivac!

CAPTAIN

Corporal, call Marble Mountain, get a bird.

(Corpsman works on Lieutenant)

All right, how bad is he hit?

CORPSMAN

Stay with me, Lieutenant, don't leave, keep your eyes open. Captain, his gut is blown open, I see lots of blood. His fucking intestines are hanging out. Looks like a skull wound, too, part of one ear's gone, and his head is bleeding. Large wounds all up and down his arms and legs. Not sure he's conscious. I'm putting pressure on gut wound, but it's still spurting blood. I need some light. He needs to get to a hospital fast.

CORPORAL

This is India, over. Need a medivac, over. (*beat*) We're about 30 clicks southwest of Danang, VC in the perimeter. (*beat*) One WIA, losing lots of blood. (*beat*) Yes, sir, understood. Roger, out.

Captain, Marble Mountain says they are standing down. No birds 'til dawn. Too dangerous for a night mission.

CAPTAIN

Gimme that.

(Grabs handset)

Major, this is India Six, got a lieutenant losing lots of blood. Took an RPG in the gut. We need a medivac fast! Can you get us one? The boy needs help. (*beat*) I understand, sir, but he may not make dawn. (*beat*) Yes, sir, we're under attack. It's quiet now. Don't know how many.

(To Corpsman)

Doc, how long does he have?

CORPSMAN

I can't stop this bleeding. He's got a lot of wounds. We need a bird, Captain. Soon.

CAPTAIN

I'm working on it. Do what you can. Will he make dawn?

CORPSMAN

No sir.

CAPTAIN

(On phone)

Major, he's going to bleed out. (*beat*) He's our Forward Observer. He needs to get to a hospital now! Our perimeter's quiet, can you send a bird? (*beat*) Major, this young man's going to die.

(To Gunny)

Get the Chaplain.

GUNNY

(Walks towards Chaplain)

Father, the lieutenant's in bad shape. Skipper's working on a medivac, but it doesn't look good. He needs all the help he can get.

CHAPLAIN

Doc, how is he?

CORPSMAN

He's in bad shape, Father, losing lots of blood.

CHAPLAIN

Can he hear me?

CORPSMAN

I think so.

CHAPLAIN

(Kneels beside Lieutenant)

LIEUTENANT

Father, why are you here?

CHAPLAIN

Son, I'm here to pray with you. Through this holy anointing may the Lord in His Love and Mercy help you with the Grace of the Holy Spirit.

(ENTER Woman In White)

WOMAN IN WHITE

Stay.

LIEUTENANT

(Screams

No, no, no, no! Go away!

Morphine.

CORPSMAN

Can't, lieutenant. You got hit in the gut and head. Morphine will kill you. Your blood pressure will go down, and you'll go into shock. You got to put up with the pain, man. I can't help you.

CAPTAIN
(On the phone)

Major, let me talk to the Colonel.

(*beat*)

Colonel, I know it's dangerous. But we got a Marine who's going to die without some help. Doc's doing all he can, but the Lieutenant is shot up and pouring blood. Our perimeter's tight for now, sir. We can hold a landing zone for a Huey if you can get me one.

Yes, sir, Colonel, understood, we'll get a chopper at first light. Mission first. Yes, sir. We'll do all we can.

(Lieutenant rises to his knees; bloody, he takes the kneeling Chaplain's hands, mirrors his posture, and prays over him)

LIEUTENANT
O, Death where are your thorns, where is your sting? He will ransom me from the power of the grave. He will redeem me from death. O, Death, He will be thy plague. O grave, I will be your destruction and compassion shall be hidden from my eyes.

CAPTAIN

Corporal.

(Captain hands off phone to Corporal; just before Corporal hangs it up, he hears something on the line, brings it up to his ear)

This is India Three, over. (*beat*) Yes, I hear you five by five. (*beat*) What's your position? Over. (*beat*) Yes, we're in a fight. (*beat*) Yes, sir, the LZ is hot, but we need a medivac bad. Over. (*beat*)

(Lieutenant lies down with his wounds)

(Woman in White EXITS)

Hang on, I'll get him.

Captain, got an Army Warrant Officer in a Chinook, about a click out. He was monitoring our transmission. He can see the tracers and mortar rounds. He says he wants to come down for medivac.

CAPTAIN

An Army chopper?

CORPORAL

Yes, sir.

CAPTAIN

What the fuck is Army doing in our AO? That's impossible.

Shouldn't be there.

Did you say a Chinook?

(Corporal nods)

Holy shit, that thing's the size of a house. Why's he on our freq and flying around in the middle of the night?

CORPORAL
Sir - wants to talk to you.

(Hands phone to Captain)

CAPTAIN
This is India Six, Army, what's your position? (*beat*) I see you. (*beat*) Roger, you in a Chinook? Christ, that's huge. Look, Army, we don't have much space to work with. But we got a lieutenant who's losing lots of blood and needs a ride out, fast.

Are you on a mission? That monster you're flying is an easy target. You're lucky you haven't been hit by mistake.

You shouldn't be out here. You're a miracle.

(To Gunny)

Gimme me a sitrep.

GUNNY

We're holding, sir. Lots of confusion, don't know how many VC are out there.

CAPTAIN
(To Pilot)

We're taking fire, mortars, RPGs, small arms. We haven't secured our perimeter. (*beat*) Yes, we can set up an LZ, but it'll be hot, repeat, LZ will be hot. You'll be an easy target, pal. You sure you want to get your nose bloodied in this brawl? (*beat*) Okay, Army. Roger that.

(To Gunny)

He's coming down. Mark our lines. Set an LZ next to those two small mounds. I know it's a small space, but it's the best we can do.

GUNNY

Will do, Skipper.

CAPTAIN
(On radio to pilot)

We're in a Vietnamese Cemetery with grave mounds. Can you land that big sonofabitch in this? You have a gunner? (*beat*) Holy shit, just you? Man, what are you doing here? (*beat*)

Alright, my Marines will guide you in. The lieutenant can't move and is semi-conscious. We'll carry him to you in a poncho liner.

(To Gunny)

Move some Marines around the LZ. Lay down some fire, keep 'em away as best you can.

This is suicide.

(Corpsman and radio operator shift Lieutenant onto a poncho)

CAPTAIN
Doc, get him ready for extraction. Get ready. We gotta get him loaded fast.

CORPSMAN
Be still, Lieutenant. He's coming for you.

(Bright white light shines down; chopper sounds; wind)

CAPTAIN
This is India Six, we're set, bring it down. (*beat*) No, that's as much room as we got. Ease down. Expect ground fire. They've got RPGs, we'll try to pin them down.

GUNNY

We're ready, Captain. What else does the pilot need?

CAPTAIN

(Into phone)

You want me to do what? (*beat*) Say what? (*beat*) Jesus, man …
alright, alright, fine. Yes, we're fucking lucky the Army is here
to save our Marine asses. Now get the fuck down here.

GUNNY

Semper Fi.

(Helicopter sounds, flashing lights, sudden increased gunfire.
Church organ opens in the background, builds to a crescendo
as the Chinook descends; a shaky white light shines down on
Lieutenant)

CAPTAIN

Let's go, pick him up, get him on the bird! Be careful of his
wounds.

GUNNY

Put him in the back and get out fast.

(Marines place Lieutenant in the chopper, exit and pound the
Chinook's side)

Go, go, go!

(Church organ reaches peak as the helicopter lifts off.)

Get up, you big bastard! Get out of here.

Un-fucking-believable.

Fucking miracle.

SCENE 2

(Hospital Room all in white; Sign on door – *95ᵗʰ Medivac Da Nang*. Group of Doctors surround a surgery table, Lieutenant unconscious)

(Woman In White stands off to side)

DOCTOR MOTT
What do we have here?

PA

Marine Lieutenant just out of triage. Medivac-ed in thirty minutes ago. Head wounds, deep laceration of the intestines, multiple arm and leg wounds.

DOCTOR MOTT
Okay, we need to stop the bleeding and stabilize the intestines. Hand me a number ten scalpel. He's got gangrene on small intestines; he's been wounded for a while; got here just in time.

We need to remove the transverse colon and the damaged small intestines.

                    PA
What about the head wound? He's losing lots of blood.

             DOCTOR MOTT
Get an ABD on it; we'll get to it later. We need to finish the colectomy. Open a
central line, he needs more blood. Hand me the forceps to remove the colon.

                    PA
Drains are in place, ready to open colostomy vents. I put in a new IV. We've stopped the bleeding on all arm and leg wounds. Head wound still draining.

             DOCTOR MOTT
Nurse, we've done all we can. It's out of our hands. Let me know if anything changes.

(Doctors exit)

(Nurse stands in silence, she checks IVs and bandages)

                   NURSE
C'mon Marine, wake up.

(Chaplain slips in; Lieutenant moans and wakes; he sees

Chaplain, screams)

LIEUTENANT

No, no.

CHAPLAIN

Son.

LIEUTENANT

Go away.

NURSE

Go away.

(Chaplain exits)

You're awake! Yes! Yes! Thank God, we've been so worried.

Doctor, Doctor, he's awake!

(To Lieutenant)

You want anything?

(She moves to side of bed to kiss lieutenant on the cheek)

I'm going to find Doctor Mott. Be right back.

(Stops, raises arm at Lieutenant)

Stay.

(Nurse exits, we are left with Lieutenant, alive, and staying)

END OF PLAY

POETRY

Lucky Girl

My father gives me strength and courage
to weather any storm.
Providing comfort and love,
he is always at my side

He returned from the battlefield before my first birthday,
a brave Marine warrior
He embraced me with a promise to
protect my heart forever

Friends challenged, come on have some fun
Young and fearless, sure let's go
He appears, now let's be calm, there's always tomorrow
He never angers, his smile serene

A man of faith, he gracefully led me to the Divine
Never requesting obedience,
he quietly showed me the Way
A difficult space entered my heart,
like a ghost my father appeared
The future is yours
Honor your mother, she loves you
The future challenged, my confidence weakened

My darling, believe your heart knows truth
I am always here to vanquish doubt

His devotion and respect for my mother
taught me the sanctity of love
What a gift of comprehension

Life rolls, my father means nothing
pleads the daughter of a selfish soul
You are lucky to have a loving understanding Father
I nod, realizing the gift

Middle age appears and my father
still guides my compass
My humble prayers ask peace for his soul
and thanks for his presence.

He shows signs of age and I know
his pride carries him to be always at my side
So lucky am I to have lived
with a soul so perfect

My daddy died a Marine Lieutenant, May 13, 1970, RVN
His name is on panel 41W, line 5, Vietnam Memorial
He will always protect my heart

Deception

Thunderbolts of fear, relentless rain
swirling winds of confusion
shatter the known comprehension
Terror of a passing storm?

The mirror reflects a lost image
The ferris wheel stops
Protect yourself, reject vulnerability
What do Doctors know?

Courage a meaningless prop
Doesn't everyone believe?
Tears of self pity guarantee a journey
to nothingness
The miracle becomes
a commodity with a
predicted termination date.

Long lonely walks of sadness
filled with rainbows of deceit
and sunsets of destiny.
The goal survival for tomorrow
Surely there has to be more.

He awoke to a purple and orange
sunrise of a fearless hope, feeling
the strength of helplessness.
Quiet rest the believers,
no longer burdened by false confidence.
Pleading on his knees,
show me the way.

From the shadows she softly whispered
I've been waiting for you, give me your hand
With the grace of an angel, she led him through
a doorway and guided with an erotic gentleness
through passageways of peace and understanding

He emerged unburdened by the false promise of
self reliance and eager with devotion dedicated
to pursuing the magnificent destiny of
perfect love.

The Challenge

Fate whispers
You can't withstand the Storm,
The warrior roars
I am the Storm

Fate mocks
The Storm brings devastation
worse than hell
Pride provides no shelter

The warrior grins
I am trained to kill
and defend without mercy
Fate controls nothing

Caesar crossed the Rubicon
Napoleon conquered the Alps
Pickett charged Cemetery Ridge
Fate intervened with devastation

What does history offer
demands the impatient warrior?
Humility, grace, and appreciation of truth

fate softly responds

I am the truth declares the

agitated warrior.

Fate sighs, ask the dead

Hero

Young and proud, America needed him
He wanted the best, Marine he chose
Earning the title, more difficult than imagined

He loved his wife and new child
with unimagined love
With a kiss of confidence
he went to war

Months of boredom found him on a hill of danger
Thunder and rain of unimagined power
He called in a mission of death and destruction,
lightning striking him dead

God wanted him, and without pain he surrendered
Love and sorrow embraced his lover
Confident and proud of his love,
she finally accepted God's gracious gift

Strangers

After years of death and destruction
the tired Nation quit slouching
towards the next Great Cause

Abandoning friends
to a vicious vengeful enemy,
and her wounded
to an uncaring labyrinth

Decades of medical examinations
performed by blank faced zombies
slowly defeated the veteran of many wounds

Called for another valuation
he quietly entered the small lonely room
surprised by a face of kindness

Dr. Than Duc Tho sat with humble dignity
her story of courage and heartbreak
protected by secret sorrow
Regretting the tragic history
the old soldier bowed and whispered
I'm sorry, we tried.

Staring with delicate sadness

she slowly answered,

I know, thank you

Friendship

The orbit whirls for the multitude
Alike or dissimilar, does it matter?
Existence endures for its own meaningless
Why bother with comprehension?

Man Thinks with
calculation and exploration,
truth is the ultimate passion.
We alone in a prison of introspection,
Anyone on our spectrum to share the journey?

The Heart beats with passion for things desired.
Sufferings of others a concern?
Can sorrow and loss be explained?
The emotion of compassion if exposed is
easily wounded.
We build barriers of loneliness for protection

The Society of Man pursues
fulfillment with selfish motives.
Anyone care? Seek souls of kindred
spirit to help cross the abyss.
Into my life wandered a Spirit of

grace and humility with acceptance
of the Divine. Communication of new
horizons expanded the view seen
through the daily prism of a false reality.

Always seek truth, and if found
embrace and hold it dear. Ever identify
with someone in Thought, Heart, and Spirit,
call him a friend and accept one of the rarest
gifts on earth.

Bringing It All Back Home

America called, he answered
Debt owed the Red, White, and Blue
Payment requiring violent futility in a foreign land

Paid in full, quiet and withdrawn
With wounds of indescribable horror
My lover returned to an unwanted story

Devoted to his recovery
Months of despair scarred my heart

Lost and praying for strength
God gave mercy
The brave warrior began to slowly heal,
rescuing my soul

The years disappearing, in quietude
My wounds still bleed

SHORT STORIES

GUARDIAN ANGEL

Tom loved being with the Marine grunts of India Company. He enjoyed their raw expressions of fatality—tough characters with big hearts.

Word came for India to move to the bush on a company-sized operation. Destiny headed them to the Arizona Territory, a dangerous area of jungle, hedge rows, and endless small villages, always contested and full of bad guys. He had no desire for medals and souvenirs; Tom knew all the fools were dead, but this opportunity to get some war stories and talk shit in the Officer's Club with fraternity brothers was exhilarating. Initiation time.

At 0430hrs began the ritual of organizing stuff, filling canteens, checking ammo, and eating as much hot chow as possible—C-rats on the menu for the next several days.

Grunts trudged to the pad, bitching about the dangerous and nasty Arizona, and why the fuck did India Company get this mission? Moaning and groaning was a Marine tradition. Birds landed to fill up with men and equipment. India Company headed out with a hundred or more riflemen, dressed in flack jackets and steel helmets, carrying all types of hand-held weapons to inflict maximum death and destruction. With his .45 holstered and M-16 in hand, Tom gritted his teeth and slowly nodded. Like a rock! Lock and load, let's get some!

Tom boarded the third chopper with the Company commander and his staff. Last night the CO briefed officers and NCOs that the mission required providing security for peasants of My Hiep Village as they harvested a huge and vital corn crop planted by VC and their NVA advisors to resupply rations stored in their mountain sanctuaries. They didn't want to share this bounty with the locals, and its theft by the villagers, made possible by Marine protectors, offered the potential of a tremendous psychological victory. The skipper cautioned of enemy resistance but not to worry due to the presence of our awesome firepower. Afterwards, the CO grabbed Tom, "I know you've only been in country five weeks and this mission will be OJT, no sweat. We all start this way—stay close, pay attention and you'll be fine."

Tom fluttered over the Vu Gia river watching it meander and knife through thick canopy. Huge bomb craters scarred the earth, memories of recent battles. Tom stared at the endless vistas of beautiful lush green, criss-crossed with open wounds of devastation, fields filled with dead trees covered in the thick powder of Agent Orange's malignant death. The juxtaposition of natural beauty and man's ugly destruction recalled Greek tragedy.

Tom landed, checked radios, pulled out maps and compasses, and got oriented. Soon all the Marines disembarked, formed up, and the long green line slowly moved to My Hiep. Tom and India Company followed a winding narrow trail overrun with brush. Sniper holes from long ago ambushes punctured the trail, slowing the march. The company labored to its destination, walking through a furnace of July heat and humidity. Sniper and harassing fire, concealed by endless hedgerows and thick canopy, tracked them.

At My Hiep, straw huts circled the compound, a poor man's subdivision. In the center stood several large huts for social and political events. Peppers and other vegetables, fermented fish, and rice dried on racks of twigs and bamboo. A single well supplied water. Small people shuffled around purposely, chattering softly. Things seemed calm and routine. Outside the village sprawled the corn field, bordered by large open spaces and long rows of 10 foot high hedgerows.

The menacing jungle enclosed this checkerboard. The mountains, sanctuary to the VC and NVA, rose in the distance.

Resting from the long, sweaty hump, Tom dropped his helmet and flak jacket. His four canteens emptied long ago, he eagerly accepted refills. Radios hissed and crackled, the Captain positioning his platoons to form a 360 perimeter. All eyes followed the FNG, trying to act like a salt; Tom faked boredom, giving the grunts a grin. Noticing that every Marine dug a fighting hole, he sheepishly unstrapped his e-tool and began digging his own deep hole. Dusk crept in and the LP's were set. Darkness fenced them in.

The next day, the villagers fanned out into the cornfield to harvest bushel after bushel of the corn. Tom plotted the map, identifying locations of possible enemy infiltration, and locked in coordinates. He talked of home and families with the CO, ate C-rats, fought the malaise and tried to stay alert. Night returned, this time filled with sounds of movement reported by the LPs. The Skipper didn't seem concerned. For sure the VC knew uninvited guests occupied their neighborhood.

The third day, at 1000 hours, the Battalion staff chopped in with resupply, got a sitrep from the CO, and filled their bird with fresh corn for the Colonel's evening mess. The S-3, fearing the VC marked the chopper's position, ordered the Captain to shut it down and relocate across the cornfield. The staffers boarded and flew to safety and hot chow. Word came down to break camp and saddle up—time to move out.

Fighting holes filled in, flank security called in, India casually formed up. Grunts milled around the large open area separating My Hiep from thick hedgerows, checking packs for unnecessary weight, bartering C-rats, and bitching about humping in the noon heat to set up a new perimeter. Helmets and flak jackets lay on the ground.

Hedgerows erupted in a cacophonic terror. Tom hit the ground, pawing for protection from his just covered fighting hole. A hurricane of sound and fury howled through the kill zone. A VC Battalion moved into heavily fortified emplacements at the tree line behind the hedgerows to ignite an ambush, a cauldron of destruction. The next twenty minutes lasted five seconds. Under continuous gunfire, marines lay unprotected in the kill zone. Maximum firepower was urgently needed to get on these killers; fear and inaction were not options. Tom jumped up, zig-zagging madly through the tempest. He flopped next to the two-man 81mm observer team. 81s, less powerful than the 105 howitzers, but light and nimble and able to get out rounds fast, were first up. Bullets pounded the ground. The two marines froze, eyes wide as saucers.

Tom grabbed their handset to shout target coordinates to the battery with no time to adjust; he had to execute with precision—no second chances. Tom then grabbed the handset from his own radio operator to call fire missions to the company's artillery battery. Smoke rose behind the hedgerows; the 81s came out fast and landed exactly on target. Get some!

The CO formed a counter attack leading Marines straight at the hedgerows with breathtaking bravery. Brothers started to fall, seeping blood. The hailstorm pelted their unprotected position. Sniper rounds struck around Tom and the FO team. Young village women got caught in the crossfire. Tom tried to drag them to safety, but the VC bullets cut them down. The 105s bullied their way into the brawl; huge explosions tore open the

VC emplacements showering metal, tree limbs, and debris into the sky. Tom, coordinating this onslaught of mortar and artillery rounds, called mission after mission, filling the sky. Finally, the VC surrendered to the continuous artillery barrage, retreating to their mountain caves. The only gunshots were Marine rifles. Captain yelled cease fire and called for medivacs. Tom rushed into the field to comfort the wounded and help the corpsmen gather the warriors for extraction.

Clean-up finished; battalion air lifted. A Husky, a tracked vehicle mounted with a .50 caliber machine gun, provided more firepower. Seems everybody got the message. For sure the VC did. Captain signaled to move out, and pointed to Tom. "Good job Lieutenant, proud of you." Confidence soared; he had stared into the eye of the ape and not blinked. Initiation successful, the sacred brotherhood offered acceptance. So, it happens like this.

Tom humped the corn field and through thick jungle into a cemetery filled with tall dirt mounds, elevated vaults to protect the dead from monsoons. In this sanctuary for the dead, Skipper decided to spend the night. The command center set up next to the Husky. Exhausted by today's action, a perimeter quickly formed, deep holes were dug, and sleep shifts were organized. Tom registered targets on likely avenues of approach and slipped into his hole for rest.

Around 0100 hours, an RPG hit the Husky, exploding into a rainstorm of shrapnel in the darkness. A hunk of ragged metal, motivated by decades of conflict and hate, blew open Tom's gut, releasing blood and intestine in a torrent of gore. Other chunks tore holes in his arms and legs, and sliced open his head and ear. Drifting into a long corridor of brilliant light, feeling wonderment of calm and peace, Tom suddenly opened his eyes. Screams, yells, and gunfire filled the night. Hell was in session. Seemingly from a long distance, the Captain screamed, "Hold your fire, hold your fire!" Order temporarily restored, the Skipper asked, "Everyone alright?" Feeling a slimy wetness, Tom calmly said, "I think I'm hit." Gunny shined a light. "My God Lieutenant, corpsman up! Get a medivac."

After several agonizing minutes we heard, "Captain, Marble Mountain's ordered a stand down of all birds for the night." CO grabbed the handset and screamed, "I've got a lieutenant that needs a chopper right now—losing a lot of blood. Sir, yes sir, understood, will do, roger, out. Mission too dangerous and too far. Colonel says not til dawn. Doc, how long does he have?" "They're bad wounds, losing a lot of blood, maybe two hours." "Fuck! Do what you can!"

Unimaginable hurt swept over the wounds. Tom struggled for comprehension through the unrelenting pain. "Doc, morphine!" "Wounds in the abdomen and head; can't do it." Helpless, self reliance abandoned, groaning in pain and begging to be saved, screams rose from a hopeless soul pleading for life. "Captain, there's an Army Warrant Officer on our freq says he's two clicks out heard our medivac call, saw the explosions and tracers, he wants to come down to extract."

Most of us live on a continuum of expectations for physical and mental outcomes. Coincidence intervenes but ultimately is reasoned and accounted for. Spiritual wonderments sometimes occasionally occur but are explained in our context of experience and intellectual relativity. What causes an Army Warrant Officer at 0130 hours to fly solo in a Chinook into a Marine TAOR? Certainly the Army didn't authorize a night joyride in Indian Country. Why get involved? Common sense requires self-preservation. Marines in the shit and a hot zone. Surely this pilot had family and loved ones desperately needing him, no need for glory, just a small cadre of scraggly Marines to appreciate any act of courage. "Get me the biggest piece of open land you can find, pop some flares to mark, I'm coming down." Captain screamed, "Pop some flares; mark the space between those two mounds."

The vessel of mercy slowly drifted down to madness. From the back of the perimeter a firefight erupted, the VC firing at the unprotected hovering Angel. An RPG sailed over the propellers. "Go home, seek protection." The Angel refused and circled the death trap. "Pop some flares closer to the perimeter and lay down some fire, I'll get in. Prepare him." Captain whispered, "It's suicide." More shots missed their target. The miracle continued, comprehended only through appreciating the source. A brave soul not seeking glory labored to save a fellow traveler, his courage and mercy changing Tom forever. What do you say to a man risking everything to save your life? Don't underestimate the grace of your fellow man, it will amaze and bring love to your heart.

The Cong punched through the perimeter, creating mayhem and chaos. The Angel landed in the midst of a Cong—Marine slugfest. Bullets ripped at the hull as the Angel patiently waited while marines placed Tom on a poncho to deliver him to his salvation. The vessel, with agonizing slowness, clawed its way through darkness seeking light. The marines screamed, "GO! GO! GO!" No one shot at this vulnerable and fragile silhouette. Finally, the ship and the two strangers reached calm waters and set sail to safe havens.

His Guardian Angel had rescued Tom, revealing the veil of salvation. Suffering and abandonment of earthly things brought a transformation. He had been saved and surrendered to the promise of the cross.

The need to talk shit in the Officers' Club vanished. Home, just born daughter, and new life beckoned.

LOVE STORY

August 1st—hot and humid in the swamps of Camp Lejeune Marine Corps Base. I await my husband's return from Vietnam. Five month old Paden sits quietly occupied with a stuffed bear I got her last week. The waiting room walls at the Naval Hospital are grey. I stare out a window.

Bob left on November 1st with a kiss and smile. He looked handsome and confident when I dropped him off at Raleigh-Durham Airport for a flight to Vietnam. Six months pregnant then, I'm worried, not scared. He has a thirteen month tour, then returns to continue our lives where we left off. Our two years of marriage have been almost perfect.

Nerves tingle; don't know what to expect. Telegrams say he was wounded at night by an RPG and was emergency medivaced to an Army Hospital in Da Nang. His intestines are torn open, he has a deep head wound, and multiple cuts on arms and legs.

Will he be happy to see us? Has he lost weight? How bad is the head wound? Will he be tired from the two day flight from Japan? Things happening fast; he was wounded only fourteen days ago.

A Major sticks his head in the room, "He's on the ground in Cherry Point; should be here in around forty minutes. Can I get you anything?"

"Yes—speed up the clock."

Paden gets fussy. A corpsman enters. "The ambulance is in the back. Come with me, ma'am."

My heart races. Three corpsmen ease the gurney out of the back of the ambulance. It's hot; Paden squirms. I see him and shudder; oh, God he looks sullen and gaunt, We walk toward him, " Here we are," I offer, not knowing what to say.

He stares, "I made it! Let me see her."

I bring Paden close, he holds her hands, "She's beautiful; looks like you."

"Ma'am," says a Corpsman, "we need to get him to his room." Dr. Frankhouser is waiting."

"Of, course."

The Corpsman roll him down a long hallway into a small room. They gently transfer him to a bed. He's in blue pajamas, IV's in his arms, head bandaged. Dr. Franhauser, tall, thin, and bald, says, "Anne, I'm George Frankhauser. I'm going to patch up the lieutenant and get him home as soon as possible. We need to check charts, run vitals, explore wounds, see where we are. You can wait outside, or, I recommend, go home, get a good night's sleep and come back tomorrow when we've got him stabilized."

"Sure. Thank you, Doctor. We'll be here tomorrow morning." I kiss Bob's cheek, he stares at me, tired and confused.

"See you tomorrow. Bring gorgeous." He grabs my hand, " I

love you."

We exit the base heading for our apartment. Paden plays with her bear making soft sounds. I realize something horrible has happened. Does he know? I want to crawl into his bed and hold him. He's been through so much, I don't want him to be alone.

We arrive at the apartment, about five miles from the hospital. I got this place to wait for Bob. It is small and fits Paden and me perfectly. We were to get base housing when he returned. Now, I'm not sure where we'll live. How long will he be in the hospital? Is his Marine career over? How long to recuperate? Any permanent damage?

The next day, Dr. Frankhouser discusses his game plan. "Bob needs several operations to patch things up and a final major surgery to reconnect his intestines. I want to move as fast as possible and get him home. It depends on how his body tolerates the surgeries, and we won't know until we get started. Any questions?"

I ask, "How long will this take?"

"Best case, six to eight weeks. We start tomorrow with a skin graft from his thigh to patch his ear and cover the hole in his gut. I plan to have him out of surgery by 3 p.m. We'll start prepping him around 1:30."

Paden and I arrive at the hospital around 5 p.m. and meet Dr. Frankhuaser. "Things went fine," he tells us. "He'll rest in ICU tonight and you can see him tomorrow." So far. so good, I think.

The next couple of days, Paden and I go to the Hospital in the morning and afternoon. The room is always filled with Corpsmen and Nurses. Paden fidgets. Bob and I have no time alone. He looks lost.

Four days after the surgeries, Dr. Frankhouser asks me to meet him at his office. Paden and I show up in a couple of hours, "What's up, Doctor?" I ask.

"Anne, Bob came through the surgeries without problems; but he's withdrawn and sullen; he's depressed. He needs to go home. He's not mentally ready for the rest of the operations. He needs you and Paden and time to adjust to the wounds and being back from Vietnam. We need to change our strategy and I need your help."

"Of course, what can I do?"

"You'll need to learn to change the bandages on his gut wound twice daily. I'll show you. It looks horrible and you'll need to be strong. The sooner you learn, the sooner he goes home."

"Okay, let's try."

We go into Bob's room. "Bob" says Dr. Frankhauser, "I'm going to show Anne how to change your wound so you can go home. Let's pull up your shirt."

Bob slowly raises his shirt, showing a chest full of bandages which Dr. Frankhouser removes, exposing a large red and purple bleeding cavity. Ugly plastic colostomy bags are attached to holes on each side of his lower chest.

I gasp, and step back. I want to scream. He looks horrible. "You need to slather Betadine all over the wound, then tape gauze over it," instructs Dr. Frankhauser, handing me the tube.

I put on plastic gloves, take a deep breath and spread the dark red disinfectant over the wound. Then I gently place a large gauze square on the wound and tape it in place.

"That was great, Anne, I think you're ready. Let's get some supplies and pack him up. He needs this."

We get to the apartment and Paden starts to fuss. "Sit down. She needs a diaper change. Her room is upstairs. I'll be right back."

I return; Bob has not moved. "Want something to eat?" I ask.

"Just a beer if we have one."

"Sure, I'll get it. What would you like for dinner?"

"Nothing, I'm not hungry."

I fix a salad and a glass of wine and sit next to Bob on the sofa. "I missed you so much; lots of lonely nights."

This isn't how I expected him to come home. For the first time I feel helpless, not in control. I have no idea how much time it's going to take to get back to normal. He asks for another beer.

"Joe Bascko just got back from Vietnam," I say, "he and Joan want to see you and would like to have us for dinner."

"Maybe in a while, I need time to think. Anne, I've never been so scared. I screamed for help. Marine Officers don't do that. It was the middle of the night, and they were all over us. It was awful. Why did I live?"

"Don't go anywhere," I whisper, "I'll get Paden to bed."

I get her to sleep and come down the stairs. The tv is on, Bob has another beer. We sit in the dimly lit room staring at some ridiculous sitcom. After a couple of hours Bob says he's tired and I show him our tiny bedroom. He kisses me on the forehead and gets under the covers. I go back to the living room waiting for him to get to sleep.

After an hour I settle in bed, leaving plenty of space for the bags and the wound. He breathes heavily.

ALCOVES

"Must be an important mission, Skip; the Colonel and staff choppering in for a sitrep."

"Nothing to do with the mission, Lieutenant. They came to document presence on the ground and get Combat Action Ribbons. War's winding down; lifers running out of time for medals. You get enough time yesterday to calibrate fire missions?"

"I'm feeling more comfortable. Why? You think something's going on?"

"No, just checking. I know the NVA got to be supremely pissed—peasants stealing their corn. They waited a long time for the harvest, then we Marines arrive to protect the villagers. They got to be motivated."

"What are we supposed to do with these giant cans of tomato juice the Colonel left?"

"Put 'em in your hole when you fill it up."

"We moving?"

"Yep. S-3 ordered us to relocate, he's worried their choppers marked our OP."

"Great; HQ comes, wastes time, grabs fresh corn for Officers' mess, stirs up the Cong, leaves canned juice too heavy to carry, and orders us to hump to new OP."

"It's the crotch, Lieutenant; every day a holiday, every meal a feast."

Around 1230hrs, hot as a furnace, grunts get the order to fill fighting holes, saddle up for an afternoon hump through the corn field to a new perimeter and dig new fighting holes. The guarantee of snipers adds promise of more misery to the day.

"You okay, Jonesy?' I ask my radioman.

"Yes, sir! Where we going?"

"Following orders. Better fill canteens. We're heading away from the river. No refills for the next couple of days. Battalion wants us to kick the nest some more. You know: locate, close with, and destroy."

"Sir, you think we're being watched?"

"Roger that. Keep your head down and stay close."

I arrived in country thirty-eight days ago. This my first operation—assigned as an Artillery forward observer to India Company, Third Battalion, Fifth Marine Regiment. I am excited and don't want to fuck up; senses on high alert.

Marines casually form up. Some have on flak jackets and helmets; most leave equipment and weapons on the ground, barter over C-rats, discard unnecessary weight, and shovel dirt into fighting holes.

Gunfire explodes from a hedgerow, weapons coordinated, sounding like one. Everyone hits the deck, frantically pawing at the just covered fighting holes.

Last couple days we encountered brief firefights, the gunfire quickly ended. This is different; the sound is not stopping. We were careless, pinned down by a VC battalion, in the open without weapons: a perfect ambush.

The forehead of a Lance Corporal lying next to me rips open like a zipper, blood flies everywhere. Gotta do something. Instinct shouts, get some artillery on these killers. I jump up, being in the surreal position of being me. I run through bullets to the 81mm FO team, knowing they can get rounds out faster than the larger 105 howitzers.

Throwing myself on the ground, I see two sergeants frozen in fear. Getting to my knees, I grab their handset and send the coordinates for a FFE mission—my first in real time.

A Major shouts back, "Who authorizes this?"

I shout "1st Lieutenant Robert H. Waldruff, 0110077. Get those rounds out now, Sir!" ROE Protocol—what bullshit; we're getting hammered. The response is quick and accurate, mortars start falling on the hedgerow.

I grab the handset from Jonesy and send coordinates to the 105 battery, suddenly noticing machine gun rounds slicing up our position. A peasant woman runs by. A gunshot between her breasts turns her white blouse crimson. She crumples at my feet.

The VC gun fire increases, screaming death. Where are those 105 rounds? Skip gets to his feet, grabs several marines and charges straight at the beast. Two marines are hit and fall. A round hits Jonesy in the arm. He screams in pain. I hear and see the 105 rounds blowing huge holes in the hedgerow. The bloodshed does not stop.

I pull the peasant woman away from the fire. It's too late—she's dead. I scream into the handset for more rounds. The Battery responds but the VC move along the hedgerow into the trees. Chasing them, I adjust coordinates, praying I'm reading the map correctly.

Fallen Marines scream from all sides of the kill zone. Nothing stops the VC and the roaring sounds. We're all going to die.

It always starts as a low moan getting louder as I try to scream. My wife gently shakes me, "Wake up, you're having that dream again."

"How long?"

"A while. You haven't done this for several years. You okay?"

"Yeah, I'm sorry."

"Wonder what caused it."

"Don't know. Let's get some sleep."

SEMPER FI

1

The huge C-141 lumbered to a stop at Travis AFB just outside San Francisco. The urgency of getting back to the states required enduring in the hull of this monster for the twenty hour flight from Okinawa. The only seat available put me between two large trucks returning for repairs; must keep the war machine rolling. The doors opened and I deplaned into a beautiful sunset of late May. After I hurried through the terminal, the "Treasure Island Naval Base" bus welcomed me aboard, sore, tired, and needing sleep. Tomorrow promised a long day.

Next morning I walked to Quonset hut forty-seven. "Good morning Gunny. Here are my orders to pick up Lieutenant Wood."

"I'll get him, Sir."

I looked out of the window at the magnificent Golden Gate Bridge, framed in a cloudless sky, and the crystal clear dark blue water of San Francisco Bay—so perfect it had to be a postcard. Soon the Gunny appeared pushing a casket, "Here he is, sir. Check the tag—let's be sure we got the right one."

The large white tag read "1st Lt. Robert T. Wood, USMCR, KIA FB Ryder, 13May70." "That's him"

"Let's get him on the truck. He's going home."

2

The trip from Treasure Island NB to the San Francisco airport didn't take long. I couldn't believe just seven months ago, Woody and I were here, Marine 2nd Lieutenants, excitedly boarding our flight to the Western Pacific. Woody had orders to Vietnam, me to the Rock. We said goodbye in Okinawa, "Don't eat all the pogey bait Wally. You're gonna make a hell of a clerk typist."

"Fuck you, Woody. Just don't kill all the Cong before I get there."

Bob and I met at OCS in November 1968 spending the next twelve months training to be Marine Artillery Officers. We did everything together: ten weeks of OCS, twenty five weeks of TBS, and fifteen weeks Artillery School at Ft. Sill. His wife Shirley and my wife Anne got to be good friends. We even had daughters born seven months apart.

Marines. Blood brothers. Best friends.

We arrived at the airport and were flagged through to the tarmac to load the casket on the flight to Arlington Texas. I wore my Summer C's drawing lots of attention in the plane. I overheard a guy telling his wife, "See that Marine? He's only a lieutenant and doesn't have a clue what he's in for."

The flight took a couple of hours. After everyone else exited, I deplaned and got on the luggage cart with the casket. Driving to the terminal to meet the hearse, the flag kept flopping in the wind. I grabbed it, holding it as best I could, hoping it wouldn't fly off. What a shitty homecoming.

The hearse drove to the back of the funeral home where Shirley and Mr. and Mrs. Wood waited. I climbed out, introduced myself to the Funeral Director, shook hands with Mr. and Mrs. Wood, and hugged Shirley. Shirley had begged the Red Cross to get the Corps to let me escort Bob home, which they accommodated even though I had just received orders to Vietnam.

"Oh, Bob," Shirley said, "thank you so much, I'm totally lost— it wasn't supposed to be this way."

The Woods, grim faced, looked at me with disdain. "What time is the Memorial Service?" I asked.

"Seven." Mrs. Wood said. "We need to go get things set up. We'll see you later."

"C'mon," said Shirley, "I'll take you to the hotel to check in then let's go see Lisa. She's already nine months old."

3

The crowd arrived early and almost filled the chapel. It was an open casket service and I stood behind the casket at parade rest staring at my friend. "You look good in Blues," I mused. Soon, everyone passed by, paying respects. When Shirley got close, she screamed, "It's not him—they've made a mistake!" She grabbed her father and totally broke down. The Woods came next. Mr. Wood looked glassy eyed and Mrs. Wood was in a trance. They got next to the casket, looked in and wouldn't move.

Finally, the Director led them away. I stayed stiff trying not to move, thinking, "I never trained for this."

We moved into the reception hall, talking quietly. From my right came Mr. Wood pointing a finger. "Your Goddamned Marine Corps killed my boy." Before I answered, he slurred, "Go to hell!" turned and left. No one saw him for three days.

Mrs. Wood said, "Forgive him, he's still bleeding, Bob was his favorite. I'm healing since Bob came to my bed last week, hugged me and whispered, 'Don't worry mama, I have no pain and am safe.' I need to leave now and rest for tomorrow's ceremony. See you there."

Before everyone left, I introduced myself to the Major in charge of the Honor Guard. "I'll pick you up at 1000 to go to the Cemetery and get snapped-in. You don't have to do much," said the Major.

4

"Sir, how did he die?"

"He was in the mountains calling in Artillery on top of an IOD tower around 0100 in a horrible thunderstorm; Charlie was moving through the Queson Valley using the storm for cover. Lightning hit his landline, traveled up the tower and fried his brain."

"No shit, lightning?"

"Dangerous place, Lieutenant, lots of ways to buy some land."

Shirley and I met for breakfast before the funeral. "We had it all planned—he'd finish his commitment at Pendleton and we'd move back to Sherman Oaks," she said, "Pick up where we left off. He really loved working for Mobile; his Texas veins flowed with oil. Why'd he have to be a Marine? They always get killed. Lisa and I are alone, I need a job, and we have five hundred in savings. I just don't know where to start. Why did he leave us?"

5

“ You know the answer—he loved being a Marine, and felt a duty to protect America. Nothing could stop him. He was fearless. He never thought he would get killed. He loved you.”

“Yeah, I know. I wish we could start over.”

“Shirley, you know Anne and I will do whatever we can to help you. I'll try to stop over on my way home from Vietnam. Woody and I vowed to help each other no matter what.”

We left for the cemetery, arriving shortly past 1100. I hugged Shirley and walked over to the Major. “Not complicated, Lieutenant. Stand with the Color Guard. When pastor's done and we play taps, walk the two flags to Shirley and Mrs. Wood, kneel, hand them the flags, and tell them, ‘On behalf of the President of the United States, the Commandant of the Marine Corps, and a grateful nation, please accept this flag as a symbol of our appreciation for your loved one's service to Country and Corps.’ Any questions?”

“No sir.” I got it.”

6

Soon things started. There was a huge crowd. The Preacher finished his remarks. After Taps and the 21-gun salute finished, I marched over to Bob's family with the folded flags, knelt, and handed over each one. Shirley, fragile as a flower, hugged her flag sobbing quietly. Mrs. Wood, not touching her flag, just stared at the casket. I got up, paid respects to each family member, cut a tight salute, choked up, and walked back quickly to the Color Guard. Before turning around, I chided my sorry ass. Suck it up you goddamn pussy, DO NOT let these people see a Marine cry. You owe it to Woody.

The crowd slowly thinned out and I went to Shirley and Lisa. "The guys are waiting. Remember, anything, anytime, just get hold of me. We'll get through this."

I turned and she grabbed my hand, "Be careful. Promise you won't get hurt. I can't lose you too."

"Take good care of Lisa—Bob loved her. See you soon."

After it all ended, Bob's brothers drove me to the airport to catch my flight to LA to spend two days with my parents, Anne, and Paden, my three month old daughter whom I'd not yet seen. They dropped me off at the curb of United, "Thanks guys. Your brother died a hero. Be proud of him. Stay in touch."

7

Our homecoming included lots of small talk and ended before it started. I learned to change a diaper, played with Paden and we all avoided talking about the elephant in the room. Except for Paden, we had been through the goodbye routine seven months ago and were not anxious to repeat the ritual, and this time I had orders for Nam and Woody was dead.

Inevitably, our reunion ended and we got into my father's car for the short ride to El Toro where I waited for availability on a flight to Vietnam. After deftly navigating the freeways, we pulled up to the TOQ. Knowing the song by heart, I got out of the car, grabbed my bag, quickly kissed Anne, my mother, and sweet Paden, and shook my old man's hand. "Don't worry—I'll be home soon." They drove off and I waved goodbye to the most important people in my life.

After checking in, I got my key, walked down a long hallway, unlocked the door, entered the small lonely room and dropped my bag. Grabbing a beer from the fridge, I collapsed in a chair and stared at a blank grey wall waiting for the phone to ring.

A WIFE'S REFLECTIONS

After Bob completed his book, *From a Marine*, I was asked several times "How did you feel during Bob's return and recovery?" After catching a breath, I started remembering those scary months or our lives.

When I said goodbye to Bob at the airport in 1968 and began my trip back to Jacksonville, I prayed for his safe return. Knowing we were going to have our baby and feeling fortunate to have my parents nearby at Camp Lejeune, I felt I would be fine, never dreaming what would happen in a few months.

Our daughter Paden was born in February and as my dad (The General) tells it, the drive to the hospital in a terrible rain storm was harder than being in a war.

Getting the call from Headquarters Marine Corps, saying Bob had been wounded and had been taken to the hospital with severe wounds scared me more than I can express. Luckily my parents helped me with our newborn. I do dream sometimes of seeing the taxi cab pull up to the apartment and the driver delivering the dreaded telegram notifying us of Bob's injuries.

Paden, my mother, and I were given the day and time when Bob would arrive at the hospital to begin his recovery. I kept thinking "God never gives you more than you can handle".

As the ambulance backed into the hospital ramp, all I could think was "Thank God Bob is alive." Being a Marine brat, many of my friends died in Vietnam and never had this chance to be together as a family. His head was bandaged, but his smile reflected his relief and joy to see Paden and me. I was in tears to know he was safe and would recover.

After several weeks in the hospital, the doctor told me Bob was depressed, not eating, and needed to go home to recover before any more operations. For this to happen, I had to agree to change his wound dressings and assist with the double barrel colostomy regimen. The doctor prepared me for the first look at Bob's wounds; I gulped and said I could do it. He sent me home with a package of bandages, telling me to call if there were any problems.

Unbeknownst to me, Bob's mother bought us a basset hound on his parents' way out of town. There I was playing nurse to Bob, mother to Paden, and housebreaking a wonderful new pet. Hands full, I had no time for self pity—this would all work out. I repeated in my nightly prayers.

Happily, we began our next few months with little drama

and Bob began to recover. Paden was a wonderful addition to our family, Emily the bassett became a Godsend, giving Bob a daily purpose, and Tucker, our son, joined our family two years later.

Anne Fegan Waldruff

ACKNOWLEDGMENT

To Matthew S. Farrell, friend and brother Marine who's encouragement, writing skills, and publishing experience convinced us this is a story worth sharing. Semper Fi.

PHOTOS

Lt. Waldruff with an 8" howitzer on Hill 52.

On Hill 52 with an ARVN ranger.

Leaving Okinawa for cold-weather training at Mt. Fuji, Japan.

First day at Da Nang.

Resupply by a Chinook at Hill 52.

First Marine Division Base outside of barracks with a Vietnamese cleaning lady.

Left to right, Waldruff, Wood, Ludman, and Schmitt playing poker
and enjoying adult beverages on Okinawa.

Hill 52 facing the Arizona Territory.

Birthday party at Ft. Sill Artillery School; Waldruff and Wood.

First time in dress blues; showing off at Quantico, VA.

Dressed for NROTC training class, first year at University of Virginia.

Last time with Lt. Wood, Okinawa.

Showing off my mustache at Mt. Fuji.

Meeting Paden for the first time on R&R after Wood's funeral.
Paden was three months old.

With Paden for the first time, Lake Arrowhead, CA.

Home and recuperating with Paden, Fall of 1970.

Paden with Emily, my mother's gift to me when I was recuperating.

No longer in the Corps, cutting a Christmas tree, Falls Church, VA.

Paden, Tucker, and me. Paden was on her way to UVA.
Tucker followed in two years, after a haircut.

UVA's arch at Hospital Drive, inscribed with "Enter by this Gateway and
Seek the Way of Honor, the Light of Truth, the Will to Work for Men."
I have a photo with my father there and also one with Tucker.

Paden, Anne, and me at Tucker's UVA graduation. He must have taken the photo.

Robert and Anne Waldruff, circa 2021.

With Paden, the first time to see a play at Firehouse Theatre.
My one-act play *Guardian Angels* would be produced there in 2021.

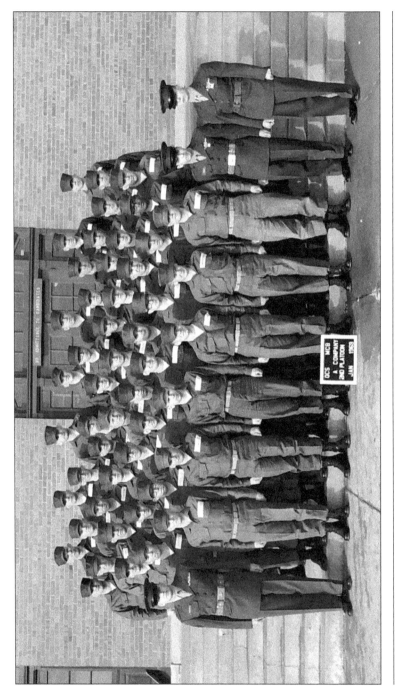

OCS Platoon photo of OCS class January 1969, right before graduation. Dennis Mrockzkowski is second row from the top, third from the left. Bob Wood is top row, first on the right. I'm third row from the top, fifth from the right.

CPSIA information can be obtained
at www.ICGtesting.com
Printed in the USA
BVHW031308201121
621900BV00005B/16